New Lives

Stories of Rescued Dogs
Helping, Healing and Giving Hope

Joanne Wannan

The amazing ways that Rescue Dogs
are being used in a healing capacity,
Changing both Human – and Canine – Lives

Foreword by
Dr. Marty Becker
"America's Veterinarian"
and author/co-author of
17 books including
The Healing Power of Pets
and *Chicken Soup for the
Dog Lover's Soul*

New Lives: Stories of Rescued Dogs Helping, Healing, and Giving Hope
© 2010 Joanne Wannan. All Rights Reserved.

Published by:
3BlackDogs
www.3BlackDogs.org

ISBN 978-0-9813966-0-6

Printed in the United States of America.

Book and cover design by Darlene and Dan Swanson of Van-garde Imagery, Inc.
Edited by Maggie Airncliffe

In Memory of Haida
And in honor of the countless dogs still awaiting homes.

Haida (Photo: Adrian Gannicott)

Contents

Foreword

By Dr. Marty Becker

The idea for this book began with the author asking a simple question: How can rescued dogs change lives?

As an animal-aficionado, I have on my bookshelf numerous books on animal therapy. There are also many books that tell heartwarming stories about rescued dogs. But *NEW LIVES: Stories of Rescued Dogs Helping, Healing and Giving Hope* is the only book that looks at the important intersection of these two topics. It tells stories from the point of view of those that matter most – the people who have experienced the healing power of animals first-hand.

The healing relationship that exists between people and dogs is very real and very powerful. Many lives have been changed by this special connection, which I often refer to as "the bond." And nowhere is this "affection connection" more evident, than when the dogs have been rescued from helpless situations such as shelters, where they faced almost certain death.

NEW LIVES tells of dogs that work with the physically and emotionally disabled, with people in nursing homes and hospitals, and those who are incarcerated; dogs that teach children to read, provide comfort to trauma victims, and become a grieving child's best friend.

It is a sad fact that eight million animals are surrendered to shelters annually. Sadder still, about half of these animals will not make it out alive. Yet these dogs have incredible potential as helpers, healers and friends.

Many people believe that dogs are in shelters because they are dangerous and misbehaved. This is not the case. There are shelters in every city and town across the United States. For most of the animals, their "crime" is simple; they are not wanted. They are not violent biters or threats to society. They are not badly behaved. They are there because a child became bored with them or moved on to college, a man grew tired of the expense of treating a medical condition, a woman finally had the baby she'd always wanted and no longer "needed" the dog. More recently, with the current economic crisis, a startling number of dogs are placed in shelters because a family lost their home due to a financial disaster or mortgage foreclosure.

Another common misconception is that only mutts and senior dogs end up in shelters. In fact, many abandoned and displaced dogs are young, and up to 30 percent of those in shelters are purebreds. There are also rescue groups for every conceivable breed of dog, from Labrador retrievers and poodles, to rarer breeds like the xoloitzcuintli (Mexican hairless). Homelessness in animals is truly indiscriminate.

Joanne Wannan is an animal advocate whose household includes Emma, a rescued dog. She knows first-hand the joy and healing that animals can provide, having long been involved in activities such as visiting hospitals and nursing homes with her "therapy dog." Joanne takes the reader on an incredible journey filled with hope and healing, where they will discover the amazing things that rescue dogs can do. They will meet incredible people and remarkable dogs, and see how new lives are created for them both.

This book will appeal to animal lovers of all ages, to those interested in learning about animal therapy and to those who advocate for shelter dogs. But mostly, it will appeal to anyone who loves a heartwarming story, where the underdog triumphs in the end.

I used to close a radio show by lifting my voice and saying this axiom, "There's only one greatest pet in the world and every family has it." After reading this book you'll want to hug your pets, pledge to help more shelter pets find a "forever home" and harness the healing power of pets evermore.

Dr. Becker is a renowned veterinarian, media personality, author, lecturer, educator, contributor and the recipient of many prestigious awards. He is the resident veterinarian on "Good Morning America," the host of "The Pet Doctor" on PBS and co-author of the nationally syndicated newspaper feature, "Pet Connection." Marty is the author or co-author of 17 books including *The Healing Power of Pets* and the beloved *Chicken Soup for the Pet Lover's Soul.*

Introduction

The goal of this book is two-fold: to show the amazing ways in which dogs are helping, healing and inspiring hope in people's lives, and to raise awareness of the plight of shelter dogs.

My journey began about 15 years ago. I had just moved into my own condo, after having lived in rental accommodations for years, and was excited about the prospect of getting my very first dog. Actually, it wouldn't be my *first* dog; I'd had pets while growing up, and they were all important to me. But there is something special about making the decision yourself, while understanding that you will be 100 percent responsible for the care, feeding, training and nurturing of your new best friend.

I had originally intended to adopt a dog from a local shelter, but every time I went to visit, there were only large dogs available. I was tempted to adopt many of them, but didn't think it would be fair to have a big dog in a small, one-bedroom apartment, and I wasn't yet aware of all the other shelter and rescue organizations that assist in placing homeless dogs. So, rather reluctantly, I contacted breeders. After looking around and asking a lot of questions, I finally decided on getting a schipperke. These dogs were used for ratting and keeping guard on boats in Belgium; the name means "Little Captain" or skipper of the boat, thus schipperke.

Haida was truly my "forever" dog. All black, she weighed about

15 pounds when fully grown. I was surprised that I could love this little bundle of fur so much. She quickly became like an appendage to me. When she was young, she accompanied me on Sunday afternoon visits to an elderly friend. Seeing how much my friend looked forward to spending time with Haida made me realize the positive impact a non-judgmental, loving animal can have on someone's life. So we began volunteering by visiting with seniors in the hospital, and that's how Haida began her career as a "therapy" dog.

Haida was funny and smart, loyal and loving, the most incredible companion and friend. I have many cherished memories of the 12 years we spent together: the countless walks and playing in the snow. The time she snuck away with a hot dog at a cookout, and when she stole a huge chocolate-chip cookie from the coffee table, ate the cookie part and spit out the chocolate bits, as if she knew they weren't good for her.

When Haida developed cancer, I was devastated. Somehow I had expected her to live forever. Oh, how I wanted her to! Dealing with her illness and death was one of the most painful times of my life. But as so often happens, something positive came from this experience, and I was led in an unexpected direction.

On one of my final visits to the veterinary hospital with Haida, I encountered a woman who, upon seeing the distraught look on my face, intuitively reached out and hugged me, without even knowing my name. This woman shared her story of how she had lost her beloved rottweiler to cancer. She felt there was no more fitting way to honor the memory of her much-loved companion, than to adopt another rottweiler from a shelter; one that would otherwise not have a home.

I was very touched by this meeting, and by the beauty of her gesture in memory of her dog, but I didn't think this was something I'd be able to do. Haida was such an amazing companion and I had fallen in love with schipperkes. I wondered if it would be possible to find such an unusual breed at a shelter.

After doing extensive research on the Internet, I contacted, and then met, two wonderful people: Sam Ebbert and her husband, Bob Grove. Sam is the coordinator of the Schipperke Rescue of Oregon. When a "skip" lands in a nearby shelter, or an owner needs to surrender a dog, Sam will often be contacted for her assistance in helping find it a good home. In the meantime, the dogs are fostered at Sam and Bob's, where they have the run of the house and the fenced-in acre of land. There is good food, plenty of treats and an abundance of love, along with veterinary care, behavioral assessment and if needed, re-socialization and retraining.

At any one time, Sam and Bob can have several foster dogs at their home – primarily purebred schipperkes, occasional "skip" crosses, and sometimes what Sam calls "skip wannabes." As she puts it, "If a dog is black and weighs less than 25 pounds, they give us a call."

Sam and Bob are incredibly dedicated. Sam's days off from work are spent driving long distances to bring dogs into rescue, to meet potential adopters in their homes and, once the adopters are approved, to place a dog. Bob holds down the fort while Sam is away. Like scores of others who are committed to animal rescue, they spend a significant amount of time, energy and their own money to help and protect dogs that might not otherwise survive.

Through Sam, I adopted Emma, a gem of a dog. Emma is tiny, even for a schipperke, and weighs only 10 pounds. She was found trotting down a busy highway in the pouring rain and was in deplorable condition, with scraggly, matted fur and a bad case of pneumonia. Emma was picked up by Animal Control and taken to a shelter, then spent several months in foster care before she was ready to be "re-homed."

Emma was very shy with people and not used to attention and love, but every day she has grown more secure, and has blossomed. Her fur has grown into a luscious, shiny coat and people constantly tell me what a beautiful dog she is. Emma soon started to join me on my visits to a Senior's Center. For some residents, a visit from her is the highlight of their week. Even though she is still somewhat reserved, it turns out that she is a wonderful "therapy" dog in her own right.

I wondered how many other unwanted, abandoned dogs were waiting for the opportunity to make a difference in someone's life. What started as little more than a belief in the healing power of animals, led me to extensive research, and interviews with over a hundred individuals and organizations that graciously supported this book.

I was touched by the stories I heard about the amazing ways that people and rescue animals work together to create *NEW LIVES* for both. I am deeply grateful for those who opened their hearts, and generously shared their hopes and dreams, laughter and tears. These are truly inspiring stories of dogs that were once "throwaways," and of the lives they have changed.

PART ONE

Animal-Assisted Therapy

A growing number of professionals, including physical and occupational therapists, teachers and social workers, are incorporating animals into their practice in exciting and innovative ways. These interventions are referred to as animal-assisted therapy (AAT). They are goal-directed, part of a treatment plan, and have measurable results.

Take Mavis, for example. Mavis is a senior who suffered a stroke. When her physical therapist brought a dog into her sessions, she was surprised. What Mavis didn't realize was that by petting the dog, she was using atrophied muscles and rebuilding strength.

Professionals incorporate both rescued and non-rescued dogs in their practices, but many prefer the former. They feel it helps create a potent bond between client and dog. This is particularly true when working with children and teens. Those who have experienced abandonment or abuse can often relate more easily to a dog with a similar past. Children with behavioral problems often "see themselves" in dogs who have few social skills, and who are learning, like themselves, to be valued members of society. Rescued dogs can also teach important lessons about the humane treatment of animals, as well as tolerance, patience and respect.

In this section, you will meet a number of very special rescued dogs who are making an important impact on human lives through animal-assisted therapy.

Marley (Photo: Alison Levy)

Marley's Story

Six-year-old Jenny sits cross-legged on the floor, staring at the large, blank piece of butcher paper in front of her. She is freckle-faced, dressed in an oversized sweatshirt and baggy blue jeans. Jenny crinkles her nose and anxiously tugs at a loose strand of hair.

Marley, a 60-pound flat-coated retriever/border collie cross, comes over and sits down beside Jenny, snuggling close and placing his head in her lap. Jenny reaches out and scratches Marley behind the ears. Then she takes a deep breath, picks up a giant crayon and begins to tackle her assignment – drawing her "life map."

Jenny is in foster care. The life map is her story, from the time she was born up to the present. Some children use a time line approach to this project; others draw pictures in clusters to illustrate family, school and friends. But Jenny has something different in mind. She draws a huge sun in the middle of the paper. The happier parts of her life are represented by sunbeams streaming out across the page. During the unhappy times there are no sunbeams, only black footprints. Her life begins with dark footprints, followed by rays of sunlight, then darkness again.

Jenny runs her fingers through Marley's thick fur, reassured by the special bond that they share. She has read a book about his life written by Alison Levy, a social worker who provides animal-assisted interactions to children in Denver, Colorado. Like Jenny, Marley has experienced the dark footprints of abuse and neglect. In many ways, the story mirrors her own. Marley's story begins like this:

> *When I was little, my family didn't care for me. No one played with me, and I spent all my time outdoors – even in the rain. I never got to take a bath or have much food to eat. I was very lonely.*
>
> *One day I got loose. I was all alone and got into a fight with a big dog. He bit me on the top of my head and it started to bleed.*
>
> *The next thing I knew, a man I had never seen before put me in a crate and into a van. "Where are we going?" I asked myself. "Is he taking me to a new home?"*

Marley wasn't taken to a new home; but to a shelter. By this time, his fur was so matted, it was almost in dreadlocks.

> *They called me Marley, after Bob Marley. I guess his hair did look a lot like mine.*

Marley was rescued from the shelter by Freedom Service Dogs Inc. and trained at their facility as an assistance dog. But because Marley is a boisterous, free-spirited dog who loves chasing rabbits and squirrels and is constantly pulling on his leash, he just couldn't pass his certification exam.

Meanwhile Alison was studying for her Master's degree in social work (MSW) from the University of Denver, with a certificate in animal-assisted social work (AASW). Freedom Service Dogs Inc. partners with the university, placing dogs that don't graduate as assistance dogs with the students working towards their degree. Alison was paired with Marley; the two trained together for a year, then graduated as a team.

Alison now works for the Rocky Mountain Children's Law Center, providing ongoing support for children between the ages of six and 16, who, like Jenny, are in foster care. Marley is an integral part of her practice, helping children develop social skills and learn anger management and interpersonal skills. Marley's story has a happy ending.

> *Alison loves me, and I get to play with her all day. I even get to go to work with her. Alison knows a lot of cool people that I get to be friends with too.*
>
> *I get to play with Alison's friends if they don't hit me, pull my tail, or yell at me. Alison's friends can tell me stories, teach me new tricks, give me a bath and lots of other things.*
>
> *I hope you liked my story and would like to spend time with me.*

Marley has clearly found his niche, even if he *is* still boisterous and pulls on his leash. In fact he has two very distinct personalities. At home he loves running around, playing fetch and sitting in mud puddles. "He's a big old mutt, who's always trying to climb on people's laps," Alison says. "Either he thinks he's a lap dog, or he wishes he were one." But once Marley puts on his therapy vest, he knows he's working, and becomes very calm. He seems to know what needs to be done in any given situation, whether it's lying down quietly beside a child, or giving hugs and kisses.

Alison wrote Marley's story as a way of introducing the children she works with to this very special dog. "I don't bring Marley in right away. I want to be sure it is appropriate for the child to work with him. We do an assessment about their past and their relationship with animals. I never say a child can't work with Marley; but if there has been past abuse, it certainly heightens my level of supervision."

On this particular day, having Marley in the session is very comforting to Jenny. Knowing his history allows Jenny to be open and

Alison and Marley (Photo: Matt Lesley)

honest, and there is a certain level of understanding because they have shared a similar past. "Marley has overcome so many struggles," Alison tells me. "He could have turned out to be a really mean dog. But he was able to let go and trust again – and that is what these children so desperately want to do."

Alison's clients are spread throughout the city. In the winter, she picks them up from their foster homes and drives them to a local community center, church, or school for their sessions. In the summer, she often finds a nearby playground or park that they can use.

Through Marley, the children can examine their own thoughts, feelings and actions. For example, during a game of Frisbee in the park, ten-year-old Jake was throwing the Frisbee for Marley. Instead of returning the Frisbee to him, Marley was taking it to Alison. Jake was visibly upset and couldn't understand the reason for this. Alison explained to Jake that Marley didn't know him and wasn't sure how to act around him yet. "I let him know it was Marley's way of testing him, the same way Jake tests people. A lot of children, when they go into a new foster home, test the situation to make sure they are safe; to make sure that people aren't going to get mad at them or give up on them when they don't do something the first time they're asked."

By the end of the session, it was a very different situation. Marley had learned that he could trust Jake. He was bringing back the Frisbee and handing it to the very pleased and excited boy.

On another occasion, while working with eight-year-old Lisa, Alison wanted to discuss how feelings manifest themselves in the body. Lisa was resistant to talk about herself, so Alison drew a giant chalk picture of Marley on the sidewalk and asked Lisa to color in where she thought he felt anger, sadness and fear in his body. This was a transition point in Lisa's healing, and enabled her to get in touch with her own emotions in a safe, non-threatening way.

Alison also worked with Lisa on developing interpersonal relationships. Lisa had been bumped around between numerous foster homes and as a result, had never made a single friend at school. Alison had Lisa teach Marley new tricks, while emphasizing social skills such as saying "please" and "thank you."

Other times, Alison has children teach Marley tricks as a way of developing patience, respect and self-control. In doing so, they learn to identify non-verbal cues and gain valuable insight into how their actions influence other people. For instance, if a child becomes angry or upset, Marley will back away. "How do you think he feels?" Alison will then ask. "And how do you think people feel when you treat them that way?" The children also experience success when Marley learns something new. For some, it is the first accomplishment they have ever had.

Each child is different, and the relationship they establish with Marley is unique. Often, the children have not had any positive role models, and little or no opportunity to show affection in appropriate ways. With Marley, they can be vulnerable. He won't laugh or make fun of them, or turn them away. Some children spend an entire session just petting him and holding him tight.

One of the most poignant experiences for Alison was working with four siblings, between the ages of seven and 11. They had been separated from their biological father because of abuse, and were living in a transitional home with their mother, who was involved in a treatment plan.

Alison worked with the siblings for about 12 weeks. Initially, there was a very unhealthy family dynamic. The children had a lot of anger and aggression not only towards each other, but towards their mother. During the first session, Alison met them in a park. "I was talking to the mother and the children were all over the place, acting up and totally out of control. For no reason whatsoever, one of the boys ran over, kicked his mother in the shins and then ran away."

Alison had the children teach Marley tricks, as a way of developing pro-social skills. While one of them worked directly with Marley, the others would watch and record how often their sibling used positive skills and put a marker into a bucket for each positive interaction. Every time the child teaching Marley used negative skills, a marker was removed. (The one who was working with Marley was not allowed to put a marker in, or take one out.) In this way, the siblings learned to identify positive skills in each other, and to give and receive recognition. They also learned to work together towards a common goal because when the bucket was filled, they all earned a reward. These skills could then be transferred back into their everyday lives.

The change in the children's behavior was remarkable. "They learned to love Marley, and understand what kindness looks like. It was a very powerful thing," Alison says. "They were able to succeed and grow as people. They became more polite and positive, and were able to develop a good relationship with each other and with their mother." They were also able to remain in the care of their biological mother. In the foster care system, this in itself is a huge success. "The judge and domestic violence advocate attributed our intervention to the positive change in this family."

Alison also designed a pilot program for Pawsitive Connections, in conjunction with Freedom Service Dogs Inc. and Colorado Boys

Ranch (CBR) Youth Connect. Each child in the program was paired with a shelter dog and practiced teaching them basic commands. "We talked about how to be nurturing, and how to create relationships built on respect and trust. We also worked on developing positive social skills," Alison says. She feels a group dynamic such as this is important because it helps children realize there are others just like them. "At school, they may be the only one who is in foster care. Here, there is a chance to get together with others and talk about their situation, without feeling awkward, embarrassed, or misunderstood."

In addition to working one-on-one with the dogs, there are group activities which focus on understanding differences between people, and learning how to be responsible, kind and helpful. And there is "homework." A group discussion about kindness to animals, for example, can lead to an assignment where the children are asked to help someone from a different race, culture or level of ability during the upcoming week.

Kathleen Fieselman (see "Handicapped Hotel") says it is remarkable how quickly the students develop empathy. Kathleen, who suffers from multiple sclerosis, serves as Chairman of the Board at Freedom Service Dogs Inc. She recently spoke to the group about what it is like to be disabled, and about some of the challenges she has to face. Afterwards, Alison took the children outside to play a game which would have been much more fun and interesting than staying inside with Kathleen, but one young boy held back. "Are you going to be lonely here all by yourself?" he wanted to know.

Alison also schedules two field trips. One is to a nursing home to introduce the children to volunteer opportunities; the other is to a local animal shelter to learn about pet overpopulation. Following the field trip to the animal shelter, Alison shows the children a book called *A Day, A Dog* by Gabrielle Vincent. The book doesn't have any words; it is a series of charcoal drawings showing one day in the life of a very unfortunate dog that has been abandoned on a lonely road and wanders about looking for a friend. Alison loves this book. "It is non-intrusive and corresponds so well to the children's lives."

Alison then asks the children to write the story from the dog's point of view. (This activity was inspired by www.teachkind.org, a website that offers free educational material on the humane treatment of animals.) "The kids don't have to say 'This is about me,' but it allows them to express any feelings of abandonment they might have." In one little girl's version, the child that the dog met at the end of the story was the same one who had thrown him out of the car at the beginning. It had been an accident. "It was eye-opening. It showed how she really wanted to go back home and be with her mother."

Animal-assisted social work is a relatively new field, and the program at the University of Denver is the only one of its kind in the United States. Alison hopes the field will continue to become increasingly well-known. She has seen the impact a dog like Marley can have first-hand. "A relationship with an animal is a therapeutic tool. It changes children's behaviors and perceptions." Whether it's teaching Marley tricks, learning to say "please" or "thank you," or just holding him tight, the connections the children make are the basis for skills they will use for the rest of their lives.

Marley and Friend (Photo: Alison Levy)

Marley has much to offer, but perhaps the greatest gift he shares with the children is his unabashed enthusiasm. When Alison picks up a child for a session, Marley is in the car, eagerly wagging his tail and waiting to give them kisses.

Alison recently picked up Jenny, the little girl who drew her life map as a sun. Marley greeted her once, and then jumped into the front seat to greet her again. Alison normally doesn't approve of Marley jumping over the seats, but when she saw the beaming smile on Jenny's face, it was impossible to object. "These kids don't get a lot of recognition. Marley reinforces to them that they are good people and worthy of that kind of love and attention."

Izzy (Photo: Courtesy of the San Francisco SPCA)

"Izzy Time"

"I t's Izzy time!" Francis Metcalf declares, introducing the star of the live closed-circuit television show. Izzy prances on stage, excited to be here. Today Francis is going to teach her to breakdance. But first there are questions to be answered from viewers who call in to the show.

A young boy wants to know, "What's Izzy's favorite food?" It's hot dogs. Another asks, "Is she married?" No, definitely not. One caller wonders what she does in her spare time. She chases balls. And finally – a question that comes up every time and never fails to amuse, especially when you say it very fast and are younger than ten years old: "Izzy a dog?"

Yes, Izzy *is* a dog – an animated, 15-pound miniature poodle, and Francis is her trainer. But beneath the spins, tricks and frivolous antics that never fail to delight, something much deeper is going on.

Izzy is a canine therapist at the University of California, San Francisco (UCSF) Children's Hospital. Although canine therapy is gaining wide acceptance, Izzy's situation is unique. She is actually a staff member at the hospital. During the day she comforts patients, providing a sense of normalcy and spreading cheer to some very sick kids. At night she goes home with Jim O'Brien, the nurse/manager of the oncology unit and one of the half-dozen people who "interviewed" her for the job.

The idea to have a canine therapist at the hospital came about several years ago when Yvonne, a nine-year-old patient with a very aggressive form of cancer, desperately wanted a dog. Yvonne had been in and out of the hospital for a number of years, cycling through periods of remission and recurrences of the disease. While she was in the hospital she was alone much of the time, because although her mother and sister visited as often as they could, they both had full-time jobs.

When one of the case managers began bringing her Chihuahua into the hospital, Yvonne immediately cheered up. She came to love spending time cuddling and playing with the dog. Towards the end of her young life, Yvonne's mother agreed to let her adopt a Chihuahua of her own. The staff allowed her to keep the dog in her room, which provided company and helped ease her anxiety. "It was a very sweet little affair," Jim says. "It made us realize just how wonderful having a pet at the hospital could be."

Inspired by this, Jim became the driving force behind the creation of an animal-therapy program at the hospital. He talked to Lila Parem, the hospital director who oversees pediatric intensive care, and together they went to the San Francisco SPCA to inquire about getting a dog that would be suitable for the hospital. "We weren't just looking for *a* dog. We were looking for *the* dog," Jim says.

About six months later, they received a phone call about a two-year-old stray that had been found wandering the streets of Fresno. The shelter staff had named her Tizzy, because of her exuberance when meeting people, and she was being trained as part of the SPCA hearing dog program (which is now defunct). The little dog had aptitude, but she had very little interest in alerting for sounds.

For the hospital, however, it was a perfect fit (although Jim decided that no one should have to go through life with a name like Tizzy, and promptly renamed the dog). Izzy is energetic, intelligent, cuddly and cute. Her small size is an asset, as children are often fearful of larger dogs. And because she is a poodle and doesn't shed, she can go into sensitive areas like chemotherapy units and dialysis wards.

Still, Izzy needed on-the-job training. While getting hugs may seem like easy work, she had to become familiar with the hospital environment, learn to maneuver around equipment such as gurneys and IV machines, and practice climbing gently onto children's laps.

And there was a glitch: In order to work at the hospital, Izzy needed a hospital employee ID badge, which meant she needed to have a social insurance number – or at least a last name. However, with a bit of creative thinking, a solution was found. Now, much to the delight of the young patients who call into the television show, she has an official hospital name tag identifying her as "Izzy Adog."

The "Izzy effect" was noticeable right from the start. The children in the hospital are critically ill; their days are filled with medications, procedures and tests. "Izzy brightens up the day for them," Jim says. "There's nothing like it. She's the most loving creature in the world."

Jim refers to Izzy as a "smile machine." She doesn't mind being poked and prodded by dozens of well-meaning young hands, and will do almost anything for attention. Sometimes Izzy entertains with a spin or a trick. Other times she will play games or go for a walk. And if a child just wants to sleep and cuddle, Izzy is perfectly happy curling up beside them for a nap.

More often than not the children are eager to interact with Izzy, but if a child is shy she will take the initiative and engage them. One little boy didn't have the use of his hand or either of his legs, although he still had feeling in his limbs. "Izzy came in and gave this kid a tongue bath," recounted Jim. "He was the most delighted kid I've ever seen in my life."

Because children undergoing dialysis are often at the hospital for extended periods of time, the hospital has its own little school district, and provides certified teachers to help them keep up with their studies. What better way to spend recess than with a dog. Izzy also provides a distraction for children who are going through pain-

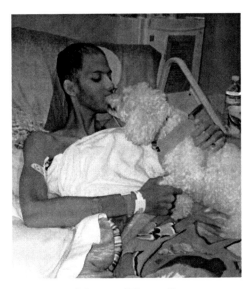

Izzy and Patient (Photo: Courtesy
of the San Francisco SPCA)

ful procedures, like having an IV started, or a lumbar puncture done. She eases anxiety, makes time pass more quickly and turns a scary situation into time spent with a furry friend. Izzy even visits a young boy born with immuno-deficiency ("bubble boy disease"). She presses her nose and her paws against the glass partition, which brings a smile to the young boy's face. "Izzy is a social butterfly," says Jim. "She doesn't have a mean bone in her body. She is all about people and what's going on."

Izzy is equally popular with the staff. A hospital can be an extremely stressful work environment; petting Izzy and laughing at her antics is often the perfect antidote. Parents of the patients benefit as well. One mother picked up this little dog and cradled her like a baby. She had been missing the touch of her son who was too ill to be held in her arms.

Francis Metcalf accompanies Izzy at all times when she is at the hospital. Francis is the founder of Friends of the Family LLC Dog Training Specialists. He makes sure that Izzy is bathed and well-groomed, and that she has all her shots. He also makes sure that the experience is positive for everybody. "She's not allowed to do anything that would be considered the slightest bit dangerous, like weasel around equipment, or get caught up on cords. She can't be an 'unthrottled plaything' like she is in the park."

While Izzy loves her job, it's not "all work and no play." She has plenty of downtime, too. "We don't want her to burn out. We want to make it fun and interesting; but we want her first and foremost to be a dog," Jim explains. When not on the job, Izzy is totally obsessed with playing ball and going for walks, and thoroughly enjoys "living in the lap of luxury" at home.

And, of course, there is always plenty of preparation to be done for the "The Izzy Show." Once a month, there is a palpable buzz in the air as children gather in the playroom to be part of the live audience. Those who aren't able to attend for medical reasons turn on their televisions, settle down and get ready to call in with questions and requests for a room visit from the star. Even staff members take a break to watch the show.

Francis, dressed in his trademark fedora and one of his many colorful shirts and neck scarves, welcomes everyone and introduces the star of the show. He considers himself an entertainer as well as a dog trainer, but doesn't mind playing second fiddle to this little canine.

Izzy and Francis (Photo: Courtesy of Friends of the Family LLC)

And Izzy is the perfect cohort. She is lively, comical and animated; she has lots of little outfits and loves to dress up. (For Halloween, she dressed up as a skunk!)

The show always includes a weather report and a viewing of children's art. Then it's time for special guests such as a candy-maker who demonstrates how to make poodles out of cotton candy, or a photographer who shows the children how to take pictures of dogs. There are also video clips of Izzy doing tricks like riding a tricycle, or of her visits to various sites around San Francisco.

People who donate to the program are invited to come on the show, along with their dogs. A recent guest was a socialite who loves high fashion and pearls. Not to be outdone, Izzy wore a faux Burberry sweater and imitation pearls. "It's a great concept," Francis says. "Izzy is like a mascot. It's silly and funny having her as the focus of the show." Laughter is great medicine, after all. Izzy's is a true Cinderella story – from wandering the streets with tangled, matted fur to television stardom and imitation pearls. "I have never seen any animal that is so happy to be alive. She just exudes this attitude that it is all about living and having fun," Jim proclaims.

Izzy may be the youngest and smallest therapist at the hospital, but her impact is supersized. Add to that the fact that she is a rescued dog. As Jim concludes, "There are so many dogs in shelters with the potential to be stars. We couldn't ask for a better animal to come in here to be such a great representative for dogs, or for giving an animal a second chance in life."

Yarn Fleas

A group of children gather around Henry, a two-year-old golden retriever with a happy disposition and a tail that wags non-stop. They are totally engrossed in playing a game of "yarn fleas." The children tie knots in colorful pieces of yarn, snip off the loose ends to create the "fleas" and place them on Henry's luxurious fur coat. Then, using tweezers and chopsticks, they carefully pluck the fleas off.

Henry (Photo: Melissa Winkle)

Henry is patient. He doesn't mind the sudden movements, the occasional poking or prodding, and the loud squeals of laughter that fill the room. And when the children move on to another activity – rolling themselves on their bellies over a therapy ball while balancing with one arm and giving him a treat with the other – Henry is only too happy to oblige. He is, after all, a dog who likes to have a good time.

But there is much more to these activities than just having a good time. Henry is actually in training to become an assistance dog. While he learns these skills, he does double duty by providing animal-assisted therapy.

The children and adults that Henry works with have been diagnosed with developmental disabilities. The "flea game" teaches them dexterity and hand-eye coordination; rolling over the therapy ball increases muscle strength. At the same time, Henry learns patience and becomes comfortable with being handled by people of different ages and levels of ability.

The games were developed by Melissa Winkle, an occupational therapist and innovator in animal-assisted interventions. Melissa operates Dogwood Therapy Services Inc. in Albuquerque, New Mexico. She works with clients who have various levels of physical, cognitive and emotional disabilities to increase their level of functioning and independence.

"Occupational therapy is a bit of a misleading term. It sounds as if I'm getting people jobs," Melissa admits. "Instead, the term occupation refers to 'any activity that people do in their day-to-day lives that is meaningful to them.' Clients communicate what they want to achieve and we look for ways to work with the person, or to adapt the environment or activity."

Melissa firmly believes in the power of animals as a therapeutic tool. "Dogs work with people who have disabilities in a whole different way," she says. "They easily earn a client's trust. They give unconditional acceptance and have no expectations. Dogs do not send subtle social messages of areas for improvement. They motivate people and give them a reason to stick with an activity for a longer period of time."

Melissa's career evolved "from a collision of past interests and experiences"– working in a pet store, as a groomer and in a veterinarian's office – and her goal of becoming an occupational therapist.

During her last year in university, some of her friends were volunteering as puppy raisers, working with dogs that would go on to provide service for those with physical disabilities. Melissa's career path began to take shape in her mind. "I started to visualize a person using a walker for mobility. It was like a video, and then all of a sudden the picture would morph into a person using a dog to help them walk instead. The quality of life for that person spontaneously changed for the better, as well. I remember thinking that a single assistance dog could replace an entire closet full of equipment traditionally used in occupational therapy."

Shortly after that, one of Melissa's professors gave the students an interesting assignment. He asked them to investigate an area of interest that would educate, or make a change in the community, from an occupational therapy perspective. Melissa jumped at the opportunity. She began reading and studying everything she could on animal-assisted interventions and on assistance dogs. Melissa quickly realized the potential animals have both in therapy sessions and more generally, as an "assistive technology." (Assistive technology is a technical term referring to any tool or device –or in this case, dog! - that helps the disabled lead more independent lives.)

Melissa developed a relationship with Assistance Dogs of the West (ADW), an organization in Santa Fe, New Mexico. They train assistance dogs who have been obtained from both breeders and rescue organizations. "That's when my career became my passion," Melissa says.

She now dedicates herself to proving that it is worthwhile to consider dogs for use in therapeutic interventions, and that dogs can be a very valuable option for assistive technology. Melissa conducts seminars all over the country. She has authored numerous articles and research papers, and is writing a book discussing the higher standards that health care providers may consider, beyond the typical animal-assisted therapy, and including specific activities.

Melissa also works in conjunction with ADW on a regular basis, both as a volunteer and in contract positions. She is an instructor and trainer as well as a puppy raiser, and houses four to six dogs in her home at any one time. Most of the dogs she raises and trains will go on to be placed as assistance dogs, but during the 18 months they spend with Melissa, they become an integral part of her practice, helping her clients in innumerable ways by providing animal-assisted therapy.

Once in a while, a truly special dog like Henry comes along. Rescued from a puppy mill when he was ten months old, Henry had been kept in a crate and isolated all of his young life. As a result, he missed out on the typical experiences of "puppyhood." He had no social skills, no experience interacting with people, and often didn't know how to react in different situations. For instance, he had never been exposed to things that moved, such as flags flapping in the wind, or papers blowing by. He was timid rather than aggressive, and would either run awkwardly towards these objects, or shyly back away. Melissa says, "Henry reminded me of a feral child. He was learning-disabled in his own way." But he is also very sweet and good-natured. "We're so lucky to have found him. He is an absolutely incredible dog."

Henry works with Melissa's clients in a very special way. "Imagine the motivation of a child who is practicing fine motor skills, using scissors to cut up treats, and chopsticks to feed them to Henry. Then consider the unconditional acceptance and immediate feedback of a wag of the tail, or his head lying in their lap. Henry makes each client feel like they are the only person that matters to him."

There are so many things Henry helps to facilitate. "All the activities are designed to help those with disabilities regain some sort of function," Melissa explains. "If I'm going to have somebody do an exercise, I'm going to find a way to incorporate a dog." For example, pediatric patients will lie on their tummies on a scooter board while Henry, attached to an Iditarod harness, pulls them across the floor. This exercise helps to strengthen neck and upper back muscles and improves posture, as well as helping those with vestibular (balance) problems. Clients with cerebral palsy often do not have full lip closure and drool as a result. Traditional therapists might have these clients practice activities like blowing a whistle or doing mouth exercises. Not Melissa. She has them blow lightweight treats such as popcorn across the floor to Henry, using a straw. This makes the activity more fun and interesting for the clients, and results in one very happy dog!

Petting and brushing Henry can help increase a client's range of upper-body motion, while dressing him in vests with zippers and buttons on them promotes dexterity. And while motivating children to do postural exercises can be difficult, Melissa has found a way. The children throw a large stuffed dice, which Henry retrieves and drops on the floor. The number on the dice determines how many more repetitions of an exercise they need to do.

Some children, such as those with autism, need to learn basic grooming and self-care techniques. By brushing Henry and cleaning his ears and teeth, they practice skills that can then be transferred back to themselves. "It is incredibly common to have a child brush Henry's teeth and then run to the bathroom to wash their hands and brush their own teeth," Melissa says.

Melissa also uses dogs in group therapy. At an integrated after-school program for both children and adults, the goal is to foster social and communication skills. Learning to groom and train a dog facilitates that goal. Henry is well-suited to this type of work. He also teaches the clients empathy as they speculate on his background. What was his life like before? What happened to him? Did he even have a name?

Because Henry is a slow learner, sometimes a child will feel frustrated if they ask him to do something and he doesn't "get it" right away. This provides an opportunity to learn how to handle their emotions and how to persevere; how to modulate their voice and be heard without yelling. "Working with Henry requires patience," Melissa says. "Patience is one of the most important things that children with disabilities will ever learn."

Like Henry, many of Melissa's clients are physically clumsy and don't know how to manage body movements. "When someone throws a ball, they catch it differently than they would an egg," Melissa explains. "With Henry, they are able to observe body language and be gentle with their movements."

Melissa also works with developmentally disabled adults who live in group homes. Her goal is to teach them how to live more independent lives. Once again, Henry plays a key role. For example, if they want to make treats for Henry, they choose a recipe, identify what items they need, make a list and create a budget. Then they decide what store has the items they need, look on a map to determine how to get there, and take public transit. These are all necessary life skills, which are facilitated and made more enjoyable by working with a dog.

At the store, clients learn comparison shopping and money management. And because Henry is a service dog in training he is able to accompany them, easing their stress and anxiety. Henry also serves as a "social conduit" because strangers often approach and ask questions about him. This helps to foster communication skills, which in turn leads to increased self-confidence.

Back at the group home, clients practice measuring, cooking and kitchen safety. These are all skills that can be incorporated into their daily lives. To top it off, there is the added satisfaction of presenting Henry with one of his favorite treats.

"It's amazing what Henry has to offer," Melissa says. "There are 50 million things he can help people do."

For the last 18 months, Henry has lived with Melissa. He is nearing the time when he will leave her home and begin a new chapter in his life. Unlike most of the dogs Melissa raises and trains, Henry won't go on to become an assistance dog because he is not great with commands. "Henry likes his job, but doesn't want to go to college," Melissa says good-naturedly.

Dogs that are released from Assistance Dogs of the West are placed in homes as family pets. There are strict criteria for those wishing to adopt one of these dogs, including home inspections and interviews. "That's what Henry wants," Melissa says. "He told us he wants to be part of a family; to have a home of his own with a big yard, where he can sunbathe and just lie back and watch the birds."

Melissa would love to keep Henry, but knows that is not her path. Her role is to prepare puppies to become assistance dogs. Still, her voice breaks when she talks about how much this special fellow has meant to her. "Henry is such a beautiful dog. He can read people better than anyone I know. He can bow, do tricks and play the clown, but he also knows when to just go and put his head on your lap to cuddle." And even though Henry is not the most adept at learning commands, "Just when you'd think a kid was ready to give up, when he was in tears thinking he couldn't do anything right, Henry would come through. He will go and pick up his leash and put it in their hands."

Melissa believes that every dog makes a difference. "It doesn't matter what type of job they have, whether they are an assistance dog, working in animal-assisted therapy, or just part of a family. None of these jobs are more important than the other. Every dog is equally valuable and can change somebody's life for the better. They have so much to teach us if we just open up and recognize the lesson."

Teacher's Pet

Shortly before Jenny graduated from the Kingsley Montgomery School in Waterford, Michigan, her "teacher," Billy, sent home this note: "Jenny excels at many things including *sit, stay* and *stealing my heart.*"

Jenny, a spunky little corgi mix, comes from a high-kill animal shelter where she used to be on "death row." Billy, aged 14, is one of the youth trainers at the school and is a participant in a unique program called "Teacher's Pet: Dogs and Kids Learning Together." The program pairs students (in grades seven through twelve) who have emotional impairments or severe behavioral disorders, with dogs from a local shelter that would otherwise be considered "unadoptable" because of behavior-related issues. The students train these dogs, and then help to find them good homes.

The program was conceived and developed by Amy Johnson, who has her Master's degree in both teaching and counseling. While Teacher's Pet was still in its

Student trainer
(Photo: Amy Johnson)

planning stages, Amy worked in the Community Relations Department for the Michigan Humane Society and became a certified dog trainer while she was there. This diverse background provides deep understanding of the at-risk students, as well as the dogs. The two have much in common, Amy points out. Many lack social skills, self-esteem, patience and the ability to trust. These common factors can form the basis of a powerful bond.

On the first day of the Teacher's Pet program, the students meet in the gym to learn about dog safety and how to recognize signs of stress in animals. They are shown pictures of the dogs, listen to their stories, and decide which one they would like to work with. There is often a sense of providence that comes into play. For instance, a hearing-impaired boy insisted on working with a doberman, even though Amy thought he would be better suited to a different dog. After a couple of weeks, it was discovered that the dog had a hearing impairment as well.

Another boy, who came from an abusive background, sat expressionless against the wall as Amy showed the group photographs of the dogs. Then she held up a picture of a husky cross that had a deformed face and suggested the deformity had been caused by an accident or abuse. The boy's eyes lit up; he desperately wanted to work with this dog. Later, when he speculated that the husky had been hit by a shovel, Amy realized it wasn't the dog's trauma he was talking about, but his own.

The dogs in the program move into a temporary "residence" at the Club Pet Too Doggie Day Care in Milford Commerce Township, Michigan, and come to the school two afternoons a week. The students teach them basic obedience commands like *sit, stay* and *leave it;* plus social skills like not jumping up on people and how to walk on a leash.

"We work at each dog's individual level," Amy says. "Some dogs are very undersocialized and insecure, so the kids who are paired with them have to start at a lower, more comforting level. Other dogs come in with some obedience training, so the students can start off with more advanced commands." The students learn about positive reinforcement skills and are encouraged to see things from the dog's perspective by "putting themselves in the dog's paws." They also do research projects on subjects such as responsible pet ownership, puppy mills and animal abuse.

Teacher's Pet provides a wonderful opportunity for students to learn more about themselves as well. Although there are no set criteria for selection, the program addresses a number of needs. Some students have poor communication skills, mood swings, or difficulty in building and maintaining relationships. Others need to work on developing positive character traits such as responsibility, commitment and time management. The program helps to build these and other skills in a non-traditional, hands-on way.

At the end of the program, the students help to find good homes for their dogs by drawing pictures, writing descriptions and putting up flyers. Then, when an adoptive family is found, they write letters to give the family instructions and tell them about their new friend. The letters are invariably charming, and at the same time, express the students' love for the dogs. For example, ninth-grader Myles had this to say about his dog, Venture:

> *He is a very special dog to me, and I hope that he will be special to you. He likes hot dogs and cheese and peanut butter.*

Loren, age 16, wrote about Troy:

> *He's a good, but shy dog in need of a good home. Handling Troy requires a lot of patience, although I'm sure you'll do well with him. He listens well. Treat him with care.*

And 12-year-old Steven wrote about Vern:

> *I hope Vern will make you happy for as long as he lives.*
> *I am glad he is going to have a friend and a house. He*
> *kind of likes tennis balls, and a good color for a collar is*
> *blue, because it looks good on him. He does have a habit*
> *to jump on you, and loves it when you scratch his butt.*

That is how Billy ended up writing a letter about Jenny, saying that she excelled at "stealing his heart." Billy benefited enormously from working with the dogs. At the beginning of the program he suffered from low self-esteem and felt he could never do anything right. "How do you feel now?" Amy asked him, when he handed her the letter. Billy hesitated for a moment, and then looked Amy right in the eye. "Proud," he replied.

Another student who gained a great deal from the program was Robin, a passionate yet reserved ninth-grader who suffers from severe separation anxiety. Robin loves animals and wants to become a song-writer when she finishes school. The first week of the program she wrote in her journal that she was excited to be selected and had two goals: she wanted to bond with her dog and help find him a good home.

Robin chose to work with Duggan, a boxer/rottweiler cross, even though there was no background information available on him yet. A few weeks later it was learned that Duggan had been taken to the shelter when he was eight months old. The reason? He hated being alone and would tear up the house when his previous owners were absent. Duggan, like Robin, suffered from severe separation anxiety.

The two worked extremely well together, Lisa Rabine, one of the program facilitators, recalls. "Duggan was such a smart dog and Robin was a good trainer. Sometimes they took a break from training and would just sit on the floor together. Duggan would even lay right on top of Robin! Sometimes he would lay there and lick her face until she couldn't hold her breath anymore."

Robin met both her goals, but it was the depth of the bond she developed with Duggan that surprised her the most. When it came time for him to graduate, she wrote the following poem:

> *I never thought a dog could ever mean so much to me.*
> *I never thought a dog could show me who I'm supposed to be.*
> *I never thought a dog could ever help me when life's hard.*
> *I never thought a dog could show me how to fade my scars.*
> *And now I have to say goodbye 'cause you've got to help someone else*
> *'Cause I have known you long enough to stand up for myself.*
> *You look at me with your brown eyes and then I understand,*
> *Why the saying has always been "dogs are man's best friend."*

"Talk about a difficult graduation," Lisa says. "We were all in tears." Duggan ended up being adopted by a family with a newborn baby. "He's doing great! Robin came back to class the following semester to mentor the new students. She's doing great too, though she still tears up when Duggan's name is mentioned. She cried at the new kids' graduation because she could feel their sadness and understood what they were going through. She kept Duggan's collar to remember him by and keeps his picture on the wall in her bedroom. She wants to write songs someday, I'm sure she'll write one about her experience with Duggan."

Another student, Hanna, was a quiet, reserved ninth-grader, and initially, a reluctant participant in the program. "At first, Hanna didn't even want to be in Teacher's Pet," Lisa reveals. "She said she didn't like animals very much and had nothing in common with them."

When the program started, Hanna wasn't paired with a dog of her own. Instead, she and another student co-trained a beagle cross. She was nervous around all of the dogs, but especially wary of Heinz, an Australian shepherd cross who had been brought to the shelter when he was ten months old. Heinz was energetic, high strung, and somewhat unpredictable, so Hanna always kept a safe distance from him.

A few weeks after the program commenced, Heinz came into the classroom and saw that his trainer was not there. He became extremely agitated, barking loudly, jumping around and trying to wiggle out of his collar. Lisa feared that Heinz was becoming borderline aggressive and would be too much for any of the students to handle. There was only one option: she would have to ask the driver to take him back to the shelter. It was something she truly hated to do.

Then Hanna stepped in. "When she saw how Heinz was reacting to his owner not being there, she came over and asked if she could try to calm him down. I was so shocked that Hanna, of all of the students, was the one who offered. I handed her the leash and stayed close by in case I was needed. Within minutes she had Heinz calmed down and focused, and began working with him."

Heinz's original trainer did not return to the program, so Hanna continued to work with him. It was a life-changing experience for them both. Hanna, who has a true gift for writing, expresses so eloquently with these words:

> *Since I've been working with Heinz, I've learned that I have a purpose, and that I can actually help and comfort a dog when I feel like I'm useless. It shows me I have patience, self-control and obedience. You can't teach something you yourself don't have in you. It makes me feel like I'm important enough to be listened to. He helps me smile when I've felt like nothing will get any better. He makes me feel like a kid again. He gives me energy and the willpower to get up and keep going. Heinz is incredibly smart. If you let him know you, he'll let you know him.*

> *Heinz has helped me with my self-esteem. I had chronic feelings of helplessness and working with him has made me feel needed and protected.*

My dog and I both have trust issues. But when we trust and love someone, we trust and love them with everything we've got, and we'll do whatever it takes to protect them. We're both stubborn and strong-willed. We both avoid what we don't want or need, but put our everything into what we do. We have a funny side, but also a serious side. We both keep trying to get through things no matter how hard and long it takes. Each day's a struggle, but each day's another step towards success.

Hanna developed a great empathy for Heinz, and very movingly wrote this story from his point of view:

Hi, my name is Heinz. People know not to mess with me. I don't need to waste my time on anything. I've learned to push people away so I won't get hurt again. When I was a puppy I went from home to home getting hit, beaten, starved and abandoned. They took me in and then pushed me away. I trusted them and they hurt me.

Since then I grew up on the streets. It was time to say goodbye to love or a family. None of that mattered anymore. What I wanted or needed was up to me. I had to dig in dumpsters for food. If I was lucky I'd get one meal a day. I drank water from puddles in the alleys. I was never promised tomorrow. I avoided humans at all costs. I still wondered if anyone would care for me again, if I was worth it, if it was possible. But just in case, I continued to hide my vulnerability in aggression.

A few months ago a car pulled up beside me and I stopped in my tracks. You can never predict what humans may do. A tall man with a cage crept closer to me. Are you

Hanna and Heinz (Photo: Rick Smith)

seriously going to test me? He was pushing it. Any closer and I'd have to fight.

What happened next was a blur. I woke up in a cage with tons of other dogs, all barking the same stressed-out and confused bark. I had no more control and that was scary. Not knowing what would happen next put me in a state of defense. Yet another transition took place not long ago that involved a room full of loving people. I tried pushing them away, but they still stuck by my side and loved me unconditionally.

Is it too late to trust again? I still keep an eye on everyone else, dogs, people and places. I've found out who loves me and I won't let them go. Love me, I'll love you. Help me and I'll help you. Protect me and I'll protect you. But once I trust you, you'll trust me too. I'll try it one more time. Please don't hurt me, please.

At the end of the program, Hanna wrote a letter to Lisa, summing up her thoughts:

Ahh! I can't believe this is the last time I'll see you. Thank you for letting me experience such a life-changing program. I learned soooo much it's unbelievable. It taught me obedience, trust, patience and empathy. It brought me joy and self-esteem. Looking back, I can see a progressive growth in myself and in Heinz. Goodbyes are hard for me, but I really wanted to let you know how much I appreciated your dedication, and your belief in me.

As for Heinz, he has a happy ending too. He was adopted shortly after his graduation. "Honestly, in the beginning, I wasn't sure there was much hope for Heinz," admitted Lisa. "Hanna proved me wrong, and I believe she saved his life."

Olivia (Photo: Sandi Martin)

Lessons from Olivia

If you go to any public library on a Saturday afternoon, you may see a dog sitting quietly on a blanket, staring intently at the pages of a book, while a child reads out loud. These dogs are part of Reading Education Assistance Dogs (R.E.A.D.®), a trademarked program of Intermountain Therapy Animals (ITA). This program's goal is to improve literacy in children by having them read stories to an attentive canine.

The concept behind the program is both simple and profound. Dogs aren't judgmental; they don't correct or criticize. This creates a positive learning environment and allows kids to practice their communication skills in a safe, non-threatening way. The result can be better grades, improved reading levels and increased self-esteem. And along the way, children discover that reading can be fun.

The program was created in 1999 by Sandi Martin. Energetic and effervescent, with an offbeat sense of humor, Sandi has always loved animals. But for a long time, having a dog simply wasn't an option. After graduating from nursing school, she threw herself into her career, working first as a staff nurse and then as manager of the Intensive Care Units (ICUs) and the Burn Trauma Unit. Her hours were long, her schedule erratic and she was often on call.

Sandi witnessed the healing power of animals early on in her career. One of her patients was an elderly woman who was very ill and had lost her desire to live. Her small, apricot-colored poodle was being taken care of by her adult daughter while she was in the hospital. This poodle was the only thing the woman seemed to care about and she missed him terribly. The daughter was concerned and mentioned this to Sandi.

This was in the late 1970s and using animals in therapy was not yet a popular concept. However, Sandi has a wonderful way of "thinking outside the box." She considered the situation for a moment and then asked the daughter if the dog would fit in a baby buggy. After seeing the puzzled expression on the other woman's face, she went on to explain. "Put the dog in a baby buggy and cover it with a blanket. Then come in the back entrance of the hospital and take the rear elevator up to the ward." Sandi suggested visiting during the evening shift when it wasn't very busy. "If anyone asks to see the 'baby' tell them it's colicky and just went to sleep – then walk away real fast!" Sandi laughs when she recounts this story. "Thank goodness it wasn't a yappy dog."

The little dog's visit was a turning point in the woman's recovery. Both her energy and mood improved, and she began to work harder in her therapy sessions knowing that her beloved pet was waiting for her to get better and return home. The effect was so dramatic that other staff members began to wonder what had happened, and Sandi eventually admitted what she had done. Luckily, the attending physician reacted positively, as did the rest of her colleagues. They even helped to arrange future visits until the woman was well enough to be discharged.

Enthusiastic about the outcome of that experience, Sandi began advocating for other pets to visit patients in the ICU when appropriate. "At that time, you needed a doctor's order," she recalls. "The physician was constantly taking out his prescription pad and writing on it: *I want this patient's pet to come and visit.*"

Soon Sandi was traveling, both nationally and internationally, giving talks on the value of having pets in the hospital. It was an exciting and fulfilling time in Sandi's life, but as her schedule became increasingly hectic, her dream of having her own dog seemed to fade further into the background.

One day Sandi gave a talk to members of the Intermountain Therapy Animals, an affiliate of Delta Society®, in nearby Salt Lake City, Utah. The group has over 350 volunteers who visit hospitals, nursing homes, youth detention homes, extended care facilities and schools. Feeling an affinity for the group, Sandi joined and began serving on the Board of Directors. She participated in fundraising events, lectured to groups and organizations, and helped with team evaluations. "For the first four years I volunteered with the organization, even though I didn't have a dog. It seemed I was living vicariously through everyone else's dogs."

That all changed when Sandi was offered a position designing a community outreach program at the University of Utah Medical Center. This would mean a regular schedule and a more structured routine. Sandi took a three-week break before starting the position, with the goal of rescuing an adult dog from a shelter, spending the time to form a bond, and beginning the training for therapy work.

During the first week Sandi visited nearly every shelter and rescue group in the state. Much to her surprise, none of the dogs she saw seemed to be the right "fit." The next week she went back to a local animal shelter with her friend, Barbara. It was a holiday weekend and an unusually large number of dogs had been brought into the shelter, perhaps because the fireworks had frightened them and caused them to run away. Sandi looked at all the dogs and was overwhelmed.

Barbara suggested they look at puppies, but Sandi was adamant. "I said no, absolutely not. I'm not going to get a puppy. There are too many adult dogs that need a good home." When Barbara insisted, Sandi finally agreed that there couldn't be any harm in just taking "a peek." When she went into the puppy section, she was shocked. The area was overflowing with three or more pups in every kennel.

Sandi walked along the row of kennels. She looked at the dogs in the first one, then the next and the next. At the fourth kennel, she stopped in her tracks. There was a little puppy with curly black hair, sitting in a bowl of water. All the other dogs in the shelter were barking, but this one just sat there, looking up at Sandi curiously. "She's absolutely adorable," Sandi had to admit. Still, she was determined to adopt an adult dog.

Sandi looked at the rest of the puppies and then decided it was time to leave. As she walked past the curly-haired puppy a second time, the little dog trotted towards the front of the kennel and stuck her paw out through the grate.

"I really think you should ask about her," Barbara told her.

Sandi hesitated. "I think she's taken," she replied, pointing to the red ribbon on the dog's collar and the little red flag on the card beside her crate.

After much coaxing, Sandi finally went up to the front desk to inquire about the dog. "The one sitting in the bowl of water?" the receptionist asked. "Oh, she's always doing that." She went on to say that the pup had been left in a box outside the shelter door. It was believed she was a Lhasa-cockapoo cross, about four months old.

"What does the red flag mean?" Sandi asked. "Does that mean she's taken?"

"No," the receptionist replied. The flag meant the puppy had been there for three weeks and they had been unable to find her a home. Because the place was overcrowded, if she wasn't adopted by Monday she would be euthanized.

Sandi adopted the puppy on the spot and named her Olivia. As it turned out, Olivia wasn't a Lhasa-cockapoo cross at all, but a Portuguese water dog. These intelligent, fun-loving dogs were bred to work on trawlers, herding fish into the nets. They even have webbed feet! That explained why Olivia loved sitting in her water bowl, something she continued to do until she was too big to fit. After that, she'd sit in any other water she could find.

Sandi and Olivia (Photo: George McNulty)

"I really couldn't have cared less what she was," Sandi says. "She was so loving and smart, so comical and sweet." She enjoyed swimming, fetching anything that was thrown for her, and taking long walks in the neighborhood carrying a stuffed toy in her mouth. Another favorite activity was playing with Murdoch the cat, and then curling up beside him for a long nap.

Olivia began going with Sandi to visit patients in the Intensive Care Units and the Burn Trauma Center. She also visited with family members in the surgical waiting rooms. A visit from Olivia was often the highlight of an otherwise stressful day for patients, family and staff alike.

One day Sandi was talking with Kathy Klotz, the Executive Director of Intermountain Therapy Dogs, about the work the organization does with children across the state. Sandi felt it was amazing that no matter what the situation – whether a child was being treated for abuse or had developmental challenges, whether they were in a burn center or in rehab – once you introduce a dog into their treatment plan, the situation changes. All of a sudden the children start looking forward to their therapy sessions. Their stress levels are lower, their self-esteem increases and they progress much faster than if they didn't have the assistance of a dog.

That night, Sandi climbed into bed, and Olivia nestled on the comforter by her side. At about two o'clock in the morning, she sat bolt upright in bed. "My God! Reading-challenged kids!" she thought. "They experience all the same things that the kids we were talking about this afternoon go through. Their self-esteem is low, and it is incredibly painful for them when they have to read out loud. They can't focus on the task because of the anxiety and it is certainly not any fun."

It is a well-known fact that most adults experience severe stress when speaking in public. But it is often forgotten how daunting it can be for a child to read out loud in class. For those with an added disadvantage – a below-level reading ability, a speech impediment, or a limited grasp of the English language – the fear can be paralyzing. Sandi knew this all too well. As a child, she was numerically dyslexic. She was terrified whenever she had to do a math problem on the chalkboard in front of the class.

Sandi has always been an avid reader and collects children's books. "I always felt bad that there are so many kids who don't read well and don't see the freedom and joy that books can bring." She wondered if the healing aspects that dogs brought to other settings could also be applied to reading-challenged kids.

The next morning, "when it was a half-way decent hour," Sandi called Kathy Klotz to ask if they could meet at a local diner for breakfast. "I told her I had this hair-brained idea and wanted her opinion on it."

Kathy was excited about what she heard. Over bottomless cups of coffee, the two women mulled over the possibilities. "We wanted to find a way to make it nurturing, fun and not punitive in any way," Sandi recalls. "We also wanted to make sure this wasn't just some bizarre idea an adult came up with, thinking it was something children would like."

The women contacted the Salt Lake City Library to see if they could test-pilot the idea there. Initially, the library director was less than enthused. "Dogs aren't allowed in the library," she explained. However, after further discussion, she was persuaded to give it a try. A four-week trial program was set up and given the name "Dog Days Afternoons."

The first Saturday of the pilot program, Sandi was nervous as she waited for the kids to arrive. Was this actually going to work? Would kids even *want* to read to a dog? Then a shy seven-year-old boy approached. His shoulders were slumped, his eyes downcast. He clutched an early preschool reader in his hand. "Hi! I'm Sandi and this is Olivia. She is really looking forward to reading with you to-day," Sandi began. "I don't read very well," the boy mumbled, glancing over his shoulder. It was clear he was only at the library because his mother wanted him to be.

"That's okay," Sandi reassured the boy. "Not everyone does every-thing well at first. Olivia just wants to be near you and hear the sound of your voice." The boy hesitantly sat down and opened the book. It was clear he must have read the book dozens of times, because he knew it by heart. Still, after every word he looked up at Olivia apolo-getically. Olivia sat there patiently, looking as if she were enjoying the story, and giving him validation that he was doing fine.

When the boy came back the next Saturday, Sandi suggested he try a different book. "I really don't know how to read anything else," he replied. But after a bit of encouragement, he was willing to give it a try. As he read the new book to Olivia his confidence soared.

The final week, Sandi and Olivia were reading with another child when the boy called out from across the room, "Hey, Olivia! I have a cool new book to read to you." With a broad smile, his head held high and his shoulders back, he raced over to Olivia clutching a brand new book he had just checked out from the library stacks. That was the confirmation Sandi needed. The program could work; she was on the right track. And "Dog Day Afternoons" became a regular feature at the library less than two months after the pilot program began.

Olivia was the perfect R.E.A.D. dog. She didn't mind noises or distractions. And she absolutely adored children – a feeling that was clearly reciprocated. It was not unusual to find a child lying on his stomach or reclining against the big floor cushions, with one hand on a book and the other gently wrapped around Olivia, stroking her fur. "I sometimes stutter," a shy six-year-old girl with a wide, gap-toothed smile told Sandi, "but Olivia doesn't mind." Instead she would sit quietly, snuggled next to the girl, listening to every word as if it was the most interesting thing in the world.

There were many interesting situations that came up during those early days of the program. People would often stare at the dogs in the library and come over to ask questions, so to prevent interruptions Sandi set up a sign with Olivia's picture on it that said, "Shhh! We're reading. Please wait until we're finished to ask questions."

One skill that came in handy was Sandi's ability to think on her feet. This proved useful when Olivia fell asleep while a child was reading. The child was crestfallen until Sandi explained that Olivia wasn't really asleep; she had just closed her eyes so that she could better imagine the story in her head. Another time a precocious five-year-old informed Sandi, in no uncertain terms, that Olivia was a *dog* and that *dogs* cannot *read.* "No they can't," Sandi replied. "But you know what? Olivia loves to hear your voice, and she loves to look at pictures. And I bet if you have a pet at home – it doesn't have to be a dog; it can be a cat, or a bird, or even a goldfish – they all love to listen to you and be with you when you practice your reading. I bet you didn't know that." The girl thought for a moment before deciding that Sandi was probably right.

Reading with children at a library is considered an animal-assisted activity (AAA). Although the benefits are enormous, they are often subjective and difficult to measure. Sandi wanted to expand the program to include animal-assisted therapy (AAT) where reading levels could be monitored before and after participation in the program using standardized testing. In that way, the results could be quantified.

In March of 2000, Sandi began a one-year program with reading-challenged children at Bennion Elementary School, an inner city school in Salt Lake City. The students, who attend school year-round, are mostly from lower income families. They are also culturally diverse, with a total of forty-three different languages being spoken, and many of them are ESL (English as a Second Language) students.

Only 17 percent of the children were reading at a level appropriate for their grade and age. Teachers identified eight students who they felt might benefit most from the program. They were between the ages of six and eleven and had reading scores well below average.

Every Wednesday after school, the children would read with either Sandi and Olivia, or with Sandi's friend Kathy McNulty and her R.E.A.D. dog, Kiyoshi. Each child spent about 30 minutes reading with one of the dogs, with a few minutes reserved at the end for giving the dogs a well-deserved treat.

Kathy, who is an excellent dog trainer, taught Olivia and Kiyoshi how to sit quietly and appear totally engrossed in the books in front of them in a very ingenious way. She cut up soft dog treats into small pieces, then placed them every couple of pages in an old picture book. The dogs, of course, would eagerly stare at the book, anticipating the turn of every page to see if a treat would suddenly appear. Kathy gradually increased the number of pages between treats until there would only be one at the end of the book. This "focused attention" training carried over when it came time for the children to read with the dogs. "Look! Olivia can't wait to see what happens!" a child might exclaim, seeing Olivia's keen interest on finishing a book.

This is just one of the many things that make the R.E.A.D. program interesting and fun. And each dog, with their individual talents and personalities, brings something special to the experience. Some are adept at turning pages with their nose. Olivia would place her paw on the page of the book while the child was reading, and lift it when it was time to turn the page.

Sandi also developed "Paws for Phonetics," using a dog's paw to break a word into parts to help with pronunciation. If a child stumbled over a word Sandi would ask, "Olivia, do you know what that word means?" To which Olivia would respond with an appropriately blank stare. Then Sandi would help the child look up the word in the dictionary, so that they could explain its meaning to Olivia. "In that way, the child became the teacher, which was an incredibly powerful thing."

Each child in the program received a bone-shaped bookmark. Every time they finished reading a book, they placed a tiny paw-print stamp on it. After earning ten stamps, they were able to choose a book from a special collection that Sandi brought in. The books were "pawtographed" by their R.E.A.D. dog and had a bookplate with the dog's picture and these words: *We hope you will always find reading to be a "pawsitive experience."*

Sandi explains that the rationale behind this is based on research demonstrating that children who have books at home are more likely to become readers than those who do not. Rewarding their accomplishment reinforces the value of learning, something many of their families did not emphasize. "These students were extremely disenfranchised," Sandi says. "Some of them had little or no furniture in their house; some came to school in the same clothes week after week. Most of the possessions they did have were hand-me-downs. Opening a shiny new hardcover book they had earned gave them an incredible boost in self-esteem. There was a look of joy on their faces when they read their tenth book and got their very own book to keep."

The initial R.E.A.D. project at Bennion Elementary School was a remarkable success. Rather than feeling embarrassed because they were poor readers, the children felt special because they were chosen to work with the dogs. They became more confident and well-mannered, began raising their hands to volunteer to read aloud in class, started checking books out of the library, and were absent less often from school. Within a year, all eight children had improved their reading scores, advancing between two and four reading levels.

The following year, on a hot muggy day in April, one of the R.E.A.D. sessions did not run as smoothly as usual. The children were restless and unfocused, as were Olivia and Kiyoshi. Sandi and Kathy suggested ending the day early and starting fresh the following Wednesday afternoon.

That night Olivia was not herself. She had no energy and ate very little of her supper. She wasn't even tempted by lobster, her favorite food. In the morning, Sandi took Olivia to the vet, who ran some tests. The results were devastating. Olivia had lymphoid sarcoma, a very aggressive form of cancer. She had only a few weeks to live.

Sandi realized there were eight children waiting for Olivia at Bennion Elementary School, and she would need to help them work through the reality of Olivia's impending death. As a trained grief counselor, as well as a nurse, Sandi does not believe in euphemisms or dodging difficult issues. So the following Wednesday, with the school's permission and cooperation, Sandi gathered the children together. She explained that the previous week, when Olivia hadn't been focused, it wasn't because of the heat and it wasn't because Olivia did not want to be with them.

"Then what's the matter?" one child wanted to know.

Sandi explained that Olivia was very sick.

"Will she get better?"

"No," Sandi replied. "No, she won't. Olivia is dying."

Even though Olivia didn't act any differently that day, initially the children were afraid to touch her. Sandi assured them that Olivia was comfortable, and that she wanted to be with them and listen to their stories, because they made her feel good. Olivia went to two more reading sessions, but they were to be her last. A few days before the third session, the beloved, curly-haired pup died peacefully at home in Sandi's arms.

Sandi was too distressed to go to the school that week, but she arranged to go the following Wednesday to talk to the children. She was particularly concerned about Sam, a six-year-old boy who came from a broken home, whose family was involved with dog fighting and gangs. Sam was always the first one to show up for R.E.A.D. and had become very attached to Olivia. He spent the sessions either leaning against her and holding her close, or sitting next to her and gently scratching her head.

Sandi was right to be concerned about Sam. Following Olivia's death, he began to act up during school. He started a fight at recess, threw things in the cafeteria, and was disruptive during class. Things escalated to the point where Larry, one of the reading specialists that worked with the R.E.A.D. team, pulled Sam out of class.

"I didn't do anything," Sam declared defiantly, as he followed Larry into the hall.

"No buddy, you didn't," Larry reassured the boy.

Larry went on to explain that he was also going through a very difficult time and needed someone to talk to who might understand. "You see, I'm really sad about Olivia. And I'm mad at her for dying. Like you, I loved Olivia very much. I'm feeling all these emotions and I'm an adult. Plus, I'm a guy and I'm not supposed to cry. Do you know what I mean?" Sam nodded solemnly. Then he crawled up on Larry's lap and began to sob.

The morning after Olivia died, the eight R.E.A.D. students walked into the principal's office. From their meager savings they had scraped together a pile of coins, which they now placed on the desk. They wanted to buy a memory tree in Olivia's honor and plant it in the schoolyard. That way they would have a special place to read – under the tree.

The following Wednesday everyone met in the library in preparation for planting the tree. Everyone, that is, except Sam. Suddenly the door opened and Sam strode into the room. He walked right up to Sandi and looked her directly in the eye. "Where is Olivia?" he demanded.

Sandi was taken aback. "Remember when I told you she was very ill and that she was dying…" she began.

"No," Sam insisted. "Where *is* she? Right *now?*"

Sandi wasn't sure what to say. There were a diverse number of religions at the school and she certainly didn't want to offend anyone's beliefs. She answered in the best way she knew how. "Olivia is buried in my backyard, with a little stone marker placed on top of her grave. As for Olivia's spirit, it is right here in my heart, and she will live forever in my memory."

Her answer seemed to reassure Sam and he accompanied the group out to the schoolyard.

The group planted a beautiful dogwood tree that had been donated by a local nursery. The children had written notes to Olivia, which they tucked around the base of the tree. Then everyone took turns recalling a happy memory of her and releasing a big, red balloon into the air.

Olivia was less than three years old when she died, yet in her short life she impacted so many people. Children left cards and notes for Sandi at the library, the school and even on her front porch. The Salt

Lake City Library sent Sandi a note saying they had purchased a book and wanted Sandi to be the first one to check it out. The book was called *Dog Heaven,* written by Cynthia Rylant. When Sandi looked inside, she saw a bookplate that read: *In loving memory of Olivia, our first R.E.A.D. dog.*

Olivia left behind a very important legacy; a program that encourages children to discover the knowledge and freedom that a good book can bring, by experiencing the simple pleasure of reading to a captive canine audience. Far from its modest beginnings in a library in Salt Lake City, the program now has branches worldwide, with over 2,000 R.E.A.D. teams in cities and towns across the United States, as well as in Canada, England, Belgium, Japan and Israel.

For Sandi, Olivia's legacy is less tangible but equally profound. "There are so many lessons I learned from Olivia in that very short period of time," she says. "Everything from starting the program, to helping kids work through their grief. But most of all, I experienced the joy that the unconditional love and support of a dog can bring."

After Olivia died, Sandi wrote *A Tribute to Olivia: My Forever Dog.* It was published in the *Courier,* the official journal of the Portuguese Water Dog Club of America. In the tribute she wrote the following:

> *I was looking for an adult dog, not a puppy, to rescue from the shelter, one with a wonderful disposition to train as a therapy dog. But when I passed by your kennel you adopted me.*
>
> *Who would have ever thought that the little black puppy sitting in her water bowl would grow up to make such a difference in so many lives in her three very short years? Well you have. And you will continue to do so through all the other therapy dogs that carry on your good work in your stead. You have left a permanent paw print in my heart.*

PART TWO

Service Dogs

Fifty-two million people in the United States alone, have disabilities. These include hearing and vision impairments, mobility problems, epilepsy, autism and chronic disease.

For many of these people, even the mundane tasks of daily living can be challenging, if not impossible. Service dogs can have a profound effect on their lives. They open and close doors, pick up dropped items, answer phones and alert their owners to oncoming seizures. They break down social barriers, increase self-esteem, and in some cases, they even save lives.

However, for the majority of those living with disabilities, experiencing the freedom and independence a service dog provides is an unobtainable dream. The demand greatly exceeds the number of dogs available through mainstream organizations. As a result, costs can be high, wait lists can exceed five years, and there is often restrictive eligibility criteria. Children, people with pets, and applicants considered too disabled (or not disabled enough) are often turned away.

All the while, millions of wonderful, capable dogs sit in shelters, awaiting almost certain death. The majority will never be adopted out, or given a new "leash" on life.

A handful of alternative organizations are working hard to change all that. They believe that with proper selection and training, these "disposable" dogs can become indispensable to a person in need. By rescuing and training shelter dogs, lives – both canine and human – are dramatically changed.

This section introduces the reader to these lesser known, yet incredible, organizations; and to those with disabilities who are already benefiting from a rescued-turned-service dog.

The Handicapped Hotel

When Kathleen Fieselman married Daniel, (not his real name) her dreams were modest: a nice home, a loving husband and children playing in the yard. But looking back on her wedding day, the thing that Kathleen remembers the most is how everything went *wrong*.

Kathleen was born in a small town outside of Denver, Colorado, and has lived there for most of her life. For her special day, she planned a small ceremony in a church close to her childhood home. The reception was to be held in her parents' beautiful backyard. Since it was early May, the flowers would just be coming into bloom.

Everything was set; the layered cake had been ordered and the catered sandwiches were made. But on the morning of the wedding day, Kathleen awoke to discover that there had been a nasty snowstorm during the night. The backyard was covered with ice and snow!

Panic ensued. Kathleen's father scrambled to find tables and set them up in the garage. Her mother scrubbed oil stains off the cement floor. Daniel put snow tires on the car, having just taken them off the day before. And Kathleen struggled to make her down parka look nice enough to be worn over her wedding dress, so that she'd look more like a glowing bride and less like a female version of the "Michelin Man."

It was an inauspicious start for this couple. Then, six months after the wedding, Kathleen was diagnosed with muscular dystrophy, a genetic disease that causes progressive, irreversible muscle weakness.

She tired easily and had difficulty walking. The doctor told her she would be confined to a wheelchair within 15 years.

Kathleen and Daniel wanted to have children, so given Kathleen's health, they decided to do so right away. Their son Michael was born 16 months later. During Kathleen's pregnancy, she started using first a cane, and then crutches. Her movements were unsteady and she fell frequently. Michael was born three weeks early because of a nasty fall she had taken the night before.

Despite Kathleen's deteriorating health, she was happy. Her marriage was good, her son healthy, and she had opened her own store selling business and technical books. The family moved into their dream house in nearby Lakewood, complete with a swimming pool, a pond with a little bridge, Japanese gardens and a fabulous view of the mountains. Not only that, but the house had been built by a man in a wheelchair and was fully accessible.

Kathleen describes her first years in that house as wonderful. She loved swimming in the pool, even though she could not get in and out by herself. Her family rallied around to support her. Michael had not known his mother when she was healthy, so helping was second nature to him. Daniel created a special bath lift and installed hand controls in the car. He was accommodating even when Kathleen's mother, who had suffered a stroke, moved into their home.

As Kathleen's illness progressed, her fatigue became constant, and her once easy smile began to fade. She became increasingly unsteady on her feet. One rainy day she slipped and fell while getting out of her car, landing between the vehicle door and the sidewalk. Unable to get up on her own, she stayed there for over an hour, terrified that she would be run over before someone stopped to help. Work became an overwhelming challenge for Kathleen, and she was forced to make the very difficult decision to close her beloved bookstore.

Daniel, who had been so incredibly supportive, began to change. He resented the countless things he had to do to assist Kathleen on a day-to-day basis; he was embarrassed by her deteriorating health, and complained about the financial strain.

Then he started drinking, and became verbally abusive, telling Kathleen that she had ruined his life. The abuse escalated once Kathleen became confined to a wheelchair. One time Daniel left the wheelchair – with Kathleen in it – strapped to the floor of her van for almost an hour to "teach her a lesson." He unhooked the garage door opener (which was on the ceiling and out of reach) so she could not leave the house. He threw furniture and started a fist fight with Michael, who was now in his teens.

Kathleen began to fear not only for her own safety, but for that of her mother and son as well. She began to fantasize about leaving Daniel, but those thoughts were always tempered by fear. How could a single mother in a wheelchair, with no job and no income other than a small disability pension, ever make it alone?

Then Kathleen learned about mobility service dogs, which are trained to retrieve things, open and close doors and assist with chores. She felt a renewed sense of optimism; a dog would allow her to regain her independence. But when she applied to a nearby organization, she was told they charged $30,000 for a fully trained dog. "That knocked the wind right out of me," Kathleen says. "I didn't even apply anywhere else. It really made me have second thoughts."

While Kathleen was in a restaurant one day, she noticed a service dog in training. She loves animals, so she approached the trainer and they started to chat. During their conversation she learned about Freedom Service Dogs Inc. (FSD), a Colorado-based organization that just happened to be located nearby. Kathleen was intrigued to hear that FSD uses rescued dogs, and trains them to work with those with various disabilities. Their motto, "Rescuing Dogs to Free People" expresses their mission fittingly

Director Sharan Wilson speaks about a special joy in working with animals that might otherwise have been euthanized. "We turn 'throwaways' into superstars," she says. "We create a whole new life of freedom for both the disabled and their dogs." Volunteers scour animal shelters on a daily basis, looking for suitable candidates. They have high standards when it comes to testing for temperament and health. The dogs should be intelligent and eager to please, neither aggressive nor timid. Ideally, they should be around two years of age, making them old enough to train and young enough to learn.

The dogs' early care and socialization is handled by volunteers. Further training takes seven to nine months, and during that time they are taught approximately 45 commands. Since the dogs will have public access, they also practice going into stores, restaurants and movie theaters, and riding on escalators.

Sharan says that rescued dogs are just as capable as ones bred and trained specifically as service dogs. "We put in a lot of time with each of them, knowing that someone is going to depend on them. We take it very seriously," she says. Sharan notes that FSD's success rate is equal to that of mainstream organizations. "The dogs work hard. It's as if they know they were rescued; that they are being given a second chance. I think they understand more than we give them credit for."

Kathleen was impressed by what she heard, but she still had a concern. How much would a service dog cost? She was thrilled to learn that FSD does not charge for placing a dog. The organization's money comes primarily from private donations, grants and fundraisers; there is a suggested donation of $500 to cover the cost of equipment that a client takes home with them, but it is not mandatory. FSD does not ask for financial information. Instead, it lets the client determine privately whether (and how much) they can contribute.

Kathleen applied to FSD and was approved. Although she couldn't afford the suggested donation, she volunteered at fundraisers and charity events, which enabled her to contribute in her own way. She felt that by doing so, she could help other individuals obtain a service dog, just as others had been instrumental in helping her.

Despite the fact that Kathleen was on a waiting list, knowing that she would be getting a service dog gave her the courage to move out of the home she shared with Daniel. She and her mother purchased a brick, ranch-style house in Littleton, near where she had grown up. "We were luckier than most people with disabilities," Kathleen says. "My mother had sold her house several years before moving in with us, and she still had enough money left for a down payment on the house we now share. We were also fortunate that the owner was willing to carry the loan for awhile, since we didn't qualify for a mortgage. Even though things were tight and we had to watch our money, we felt incredibly fortunate."

Kathleen was afraid to tell Daniel of her plans, so one day while he was at work she, her mother and Michael packed their belongings and half of the furniture, and quietly moved out.

Kathleen was exhilarated at first. She felt a new-found sense of freedom and ease, despite the fact that she had absolutely no idea what she was going to do for the rest of her life. But slowly, the reality of the situation crept in. Kathleen was 43 years old. She was disabled and unable to work; her failed marriage had robbed her of all self-esteem. She had to take care of herself, her mother and son, and Juno, a German shepherd they had rescued from a shelter as a pup.

Kathleen fell into a deep depression, not even getting out of her pajamas for days at a time. And because muscular dystrophy affects not only the limbs, but the heart and lung muscles as well, she had trouble breathing and used an oxygen mask at night. This caused her to wake up in the morning feeling exhausted, and with a terrible headache.

Then Kathleen's lung muscles weakened to such an extent that an oxygen mask was no longer sufficient. Her doctor told her she would need to have a tracheotomy; a complicated surgical procedure that involved cutting a hole in her windpipe and inserting a tube to help her breathe.

Kathleen was unprepared for what she now faced. Having a tracheotomy was a full-time job. She needed to apply warm compresses to the wound, monitor her blood oxygen levels eight times a day, and sterilize the equipment on a daily basis. The tube required continual suctioning. And because it was critical to prevent any foreign particles from getting into the tube, the house had to be kept entirely dust-free. Kathleen also had to take extra care while eating or drinking.

Not only that, Kathleen needed to learn to breathe through the tube, and at first she found it difficult to talk, or even make sounds. Then at night, she used a ventilator, which required its own maintenance. "These tasks took up to eight hours a day to complete," says Kathleen, who wryly adds, "My life up to that point was a walk in the park in comparison."

Kathleen slipped into an even deeper depression. Surely after everything she had been through – the loss of her health, her marriage, her career – this was more than anyone could be expected to handle. She could not imagine ever having a "real life" again.

It was at this low point in Kathleen's life that Inik, a trainer with Freedom Service Dogs Inc., called to say that they had a dog that would be perfect for Kathleen. Blu was a three-year-old, black English Lab who had been found wandering the streets near a dangerous intersection. When he was taken to the shelter, he was so emaciated that there was not enough flesh on his rear end for him to sit down. Despite this, he was an incredibly gentle and good-natured dog.

Inik asked if Kathleen would like to meet Blu. Kathleen said "no." Her illness had progressed further than she could have imagined; she didn't have any use for a service dog, because she was never going to leave her house again.

Kathleen was still cursing fate the next day when the doorbell rang. It was Inik, with Blu by her side. Kathleen frowned. "I told you yesterday, I don't want a dog," she grumbled.

"That's okay," Inik cheerfully replied. "I just wanted to see how Blu would get along with your other dog."

"That certainly didn't improve my mood," Kathleen recalls. "Here was this trainer. She was young and slim and beautiful; I was immediately jealous of her." As for Kathleen's first impression of Blu: "I'd always preferred female dogs. I didn't like black dogs. And I never thought Labs were very cute either. These were just more reasons for me to say *no*."

Inik was undaunted. She suggested taking both dogs to the park so they could get acquainted on neutral territory. It was a warm, sunny day so Kathleen agreed. Much to her astonishment Juno and Blu became instant friends. Then Blu went over to Kathleen, sat on her knee (as best as he could) and licked her face. "It may come as no surprise that by the time we left the park, I wanted Blu," Kathleen says. So even though it was not love at first sight, it was pretty close!

That night, Kathleen couldn't sleep. She went back and forth over the situation in her mind. "Can I really do this?" she wondered. "Can I somehow force myself to go to Freedom Service Dogs every day for the next three weeks to work with Blu?" She carefully considered the possibility, allowing herself to feel a glimmer of hope. And then, "There's no way. Who am I kidding? It's a two-hour round trip." In the last few years she'd done everything within a two- or three-mile radius of her house. She was fearful of driving clear across town. There was also the matter of all the paraphernalia she would need to bring with her. "Even if I could somehow strap my suction machine onto my wheelchair… What if there's a problem? What if I suddenly can't breathe?"

Despite herself, by the next morning, Kathleen had made a mental list of all the things she would need to do. She figured out a way to load everything on to her wheelchair. "It was like traveling with a baby, only worse," she recalls. Then, every day, for the next three weeks, Kathleen made the two-hour round trip to Freedom Service Dogs, to work with Blu. Training Blu gave Kathleen something to focus on, and she felt a renewed sense of confidence. "The rest is history," she says.

Kathleen and Blu (Photo: Patty Howe)

These days, if you ask Kathleen what having Blu has meant to her, the answer would be, "Everything." He has literally given her a new life. Kathleen's days are a busy blur of activities. She volunteers, visits friends, and enjoys a renewed sense of independence, freedom and dignity. Before Blu came into her life, Kathleen used to feel vulnerable. "Now I feel like I can handle anything," she says.

Blu has made Kathleen's life easier in a number of ways. He helps her in and out of the bathtub, assists with dressing, and does chores like getting clothes out of the dryer. He also retrieves things. For example, Kathleen uses a transfer board – a 10" x 24" piece of wood that weighs about five pounds – to help her get in and out of her wheelchair. The board is essential to her mobility. "If I can't get my board, I'm stuck wherever I happen to be – the driver's seat of the van, the toilet – places where you wouldn't want to spend the whole day." Blu is trained to pick up the board if Kathleen drops it, which she does frequently. And more than once, he has saved her from having to call paramedics, by picking up medicine or keys that she has dropped on the floor.

And Blu is one guy who loves to shop! At the grocery store, Kathleen uses a long stick to knock unbreakable items off shelves, which Blu then picks up and puts in her cart. At her favorite self-service shoe store, Kathleen points to a box of shoes. Blu takes the box off the shelf, opens it and helps her put the shoes on. And if Kathleen doesn't like them? No problem! Blu removes the shoes from her feet, puts them back in the box and returns them to the shelf.

Kathleen says that Blu is the best service dog she could ever have asked for. He is always "proper" and never prone to mischief. Well, almost never. Kathleen recalls one incident when Blu didn't act his gentlemanly self. The pair had been together for only a couple of weeks and were in a video store. Kathleen had Blu's leash wrapped around her wrist, and everything was going fine until a woman came in with a chihuahua. "Well, Blu's experience with critters that size had been limited to squirrels, so I imagine he thought the chihuahua was a squirrel," Kathleen laughingly recalls. "He took after it like a shot, pulling me with him. I hit my head, broke my glasses, and was stunned and dazed. But I do remember Blu looking back at me in shock with an expression on his face that seemed to be asking, 'What are you doing on the floor?'"

Kathleen learned a few things from that incident. For one thing, she realized she needed to attach Blu's leash to her wheelchair, rather than to herself! There was another unexpected upside: For some time, Kathleen had been having trouble sitting upright on her own. This experience made her realize that Blu was strong enough to assist her. A few days later, while struggling to get out of bed, Kathleen handed Blu a tug toy, held onto the other end, and then gave him the command *take*. Blu tightened his grip on the toy and pulled until Kathleen was sitting upright. "They now teach dogs that skill as part of their training at Freedom Service Dogs, thanks to Blu," Kathleen says.

Blu helps Kathleen in other less tangible ways as well. Kathleen no longer dreads going out in public; nor does she experience the sense of "invisibility" that people with disabilities often feel. Kathleen was reminded of this recently when Blu was in the hospital undergoing surgery to remove a cancerous lesion from his toe. People didn't respond to her when she was out without him, even when she tried to catch their eye and say hello. When Kathleen dropped her wallet, she found it difficult to find someone to help. "When I'm with Blu, people make a point of coming over to visit and to see the dog. They offer to do things for me. If I drop something, people rush in from all around to pick it up, even when I don't need them to. It's sad but true."

Kathleen and Blu clearly share a special bond. Except for brief hospital stays, they have been together almost every minute for the past seven years. Blu is Kathleen's helper and friend, a sounding board for her frustration and fears. He is an unintentional comedian as well. During a particularly boring speech, at an event no one wanted to go to, Blu yawned loudly enough to be heard by people sitting at the very back of the room. Another time, he sneezed with the force of a seismic event, which almost lifted him off the floor. Everyone in the room erupted with laughter.

Three years ago, Kathleen joined the Board of Directors of Freedom Service Dogs Inc. She wanted to give back to the organization that had given her so much. This puts her in the unique position of being able to advocate for those with disabilities. When another board member suggested that FSD start charging for service dogs, Kathleen threatened to quit in protest. "That got everyone's attention," she says. "It gave me a chance to explain the financial realities for a majority of our clients. In the United States, the poverty rate is incredibly high. We have clients who are struggling to get by on $600 to $1,000 a month, which isn't much around this town."

Kathleen now serves as Chairman of the Board, volunteering for up to 20 hours a week. She also gives demonstrations at schools, libraries and churches. And she spreads the word about service dogs wherever she goes. "There are so many people out there who are barely surviving; people who could gain a new life with a service dog. I feel like I have to help make a change in this world."

Such was the case recently. Kathleen was in Kmart when a middle-aged man stopped to ask about Blu. Just then, his wife rounded the corner in a wheelchair. She had suffered four strokes, lost her job, and had accumulated onerous medical bills. She spent the majority of time at home, afraid to go outside. When the woman saw Kathleen and Blu, she started to cry. She was reminded of how much she missed her independence, and felt renewed hope that she might be able to regain it.

Kathleen shared her experiences with the couple. Later, she marveled at the circumstances that had led to their meeting. Kathleen seldom shops at Kmart, but made an exception that day because the store near her home didn't have what she wanted. The couple had made a special trip that day too, to purchase a mousetrap. It was the first mouse they had ever had.

Kathleen and the couple have since become close friends. The woman is now on Freedom Service Dogs' waiting list. She recently told Kathleen that she feels positive for the first time in years, like a kid waiting for Santa Claus to come.

Unfortunately, Blu is beginning to experience health problems. The loss of his toe due to cancer makes it difficult for him to get around. And this once skinny dog has developed a thyroid problem, which has caused him to gain weight. After much thought, Kathleen decided it was best to let Blu semi-retire. Toby, a service dog in training, is scheduled to take over some of Blu's duties. He is from Freedom Service Dogs, but could not be placed with a regular client because an X-ray revealed problems with his shoulder joint. Kathleen has taken on the task of training Toby herself.

Kathleen still lives with her mother who now suffers from severe arthritis. Their household includes Maggie, a golden retriever with hip dysphasia who was adopted from a rescue shelter, and Jake, a stray who had lost his front leg and shoulder when he was hit by a car. And of course, there is Blu, who will always have a special place in Kathleen's home, as well as her heart. With characteristic good humor, Kathleen refers to their residence as the "Handicapped Hotel."

Kathleen is a woman of incredible wisdom, spirit and strength. Many people would have given up and locked themselves behind closed doors, but she had the courage to carry on. Kathleen modestly attributes her accomplishments to Blu, and is forever grateful to Freedom Service Dogs, who insisted on knocking on her door that day and introducing the two. "I realize how much Blu has enabled me to do, and how I wouldn't have much of a life without him."

Kathleen with Blu and Toby (Photo: Patty Howe)

A Date for the Prom

Amber Roark's high school prom was magical. The boys wore rented tuxedos; the girls were dressed in their finest gowns. The gymnasium was decorated in the school colors of maroon and white; there was fruit punch, catered sandwiches and a deejay spinning tunes. And Amber was there with a very special date: Quincy, her service dog.

It's no wonder that Amber wanted to share the celebrations with Quincy. Graduating from high school has been her greatest achievement to date. She credits the loyal husky mix with being instrumental in helping her reach that goal. "I really couldn't have done it without him. He was my constant support."

Twenty-one year old Amber is a bright, articulate, fun-loving young woman. She was raised in Oxford, Pennsylvania, by her grandparents and has lived in the small rural community her whole life. But Amber's childhood was anything but typical. As an infant she suffered from seizures and, at the age of three, was diagnosed with spastic diplegia, a form of cerebral palsy. Although the seizures eventually stopped, spastic diplegia causes muscle stiffness and involuntary spasms. As a result, Amber has trouble maintaining balance, her movements are jerky, and when she walks, one leg drags slightly behind the other.

Still, Amber made friends easily. She took martial arts classes, joined a choir and, like most normal teenagers, spent time hanging out at the mall. Her grandparents were supportive, helping in any way they could.

When Amber was 16, she faced a series of further health challenges. She contracted Lyme disease, which is caused from bacteria that is carried by deer ticks. If left untreated, it can result in neurological problems and severe joint pain. The ticks are tiny (often no bigger than the head of a pin), so Amber did not even realize she'd been bitten, and because the symptoms of Lyme disease are similar to those of cerebral palsy, her condition was not properly diagnosed for quite some time.

That same year, while Amber and her grandfather were driving home from a martial arts class, another vehicle suddenly raced up from behind and rear-ended them, totaling their car. Although Amber's grandfather sustained only minor bumps and bruises, she was not so lucky. She lurched forward, hitting her head on the dashboard, and then fell back against the seat before blacking out.

Doctors think it was a combination of the Lyme disease and the accident that caused Amber's seizures to reoccur. She now experiences two distinctive types: complex partial seizures, that affect only a small portion of the brain and leave her momentarily stunned or "clued out;" and the more serious grand mal seizures which result in a loss of consciousness and violent muscle contractions.

Navigating the challenges of high school life can be difficult for anyone. For Amber, it was infinitely more so. Her seizures occurred frequently, often five or more times a day. She was ridiculed by students who did not know her very well, and even friends shied away. "They found it scary," Amber says. Consequently, she became withdrawn and deeply depressed. "It was hard. I lost my independence. All I did was stay in my house and go to school."

While researching a paper for her high school English class, Amber learned about service dogs and the remarkable variety of things they are able to do to help those with physical disabilities. Intrigued, she contacted Amazing Tails, LLC, Inc., a non-profit organization that happened to be located just down the road.

Amazing Tails was founded in 1999, by Siobhan Cameron and Joan Bussard. The organization, which does not have its own breeding program, primarily uses rescue dogs. "There are so many wonderful animals in the world that deserve a second chance," Siobhan explains. "Many of the dogs who are at shelters are there through no fault of their own. They only need to be loved, and to be taught what is expected of them."

Although Amazing Tails is a non-profit organization, there is a suggested donation of $5,000 to help defray the expense of training a service dog. Amber's grandparents were not in a financial position to afford a donation of that size, but she was able to find other sources of funding within her community. Her church youth group held a fundraising dinner to help her raise money. She also received a grant from the Wal-Mart Foundation Community Support Program.

In most cases, staff at Amazing Tails socialize the dogs and teach them basic obedience, as well as skills specific to a client's needs. Then the client comes to Pennsylvania for a two-week Partnership Program to work one-on-one with their new service dog. Amber was in a somewhat unique position since she lived close by. This allowed her to participate in the training sessions right from the start.

When Amber came to the facility for her first Saturday morning training class, she hadn't yet been paired with a dog. Siobhan suggested she work with Quincy, who had been found wandering the streets, covered in tar. Someone had obviously tried to clean Quincy up before taking him to a local shelter, because much of his hair had been shaved off. He was such a mess that no one wanted to adopt him, but Amazing Tails realized he was an exceptional dog.

"When we got him, he burst out of the shelter, wiggling with excitement, and he had a look on his face that seemed to say 'I will work,'" Siobhan says. "He's incredibly happy and keeps everyone smiling." As for Amber's first impression: "I thought he was one pretty cool dog."

After the training session, Amber was sitting on the sofa talking to Siobhan and Joan when Quincy suddenly jumped up on her lap. Although Siobhan had never seen Quincy exhibit this type of behavior before, she immediately realized what was happening. "You'd better lie down," she said. Amber did, and a few minutes later experienced a seizure. Quincy, it seems, had been trying to alert her in advance. He alerted her to two other oncoming seizures that same afternoon.

Quincy is one of a small percentage of dogs that is able to sense seizures, low blood sugar, migraines and other health conditions before they occur. There are conflicting theories about how this happens. Some researchers suggest that the dogs detect subtle changes in a person's body chemistry, odor, or even behavior. Another theory is that they pick up on electromagnetic changes in the body, in the same way that some animals can predict thunderstorms from magnetic currents in the air.

Regardless of the explanation, sensing oncoming seizures is an innate ability, and is not restricted to any particular breed. Some researchers have tried to teach dogs this skill, using positive reinforcement. For example, if a dog is given a reward each time their owner seizes, over time they may begin to look for subtle bodily changes before a seizure occurs. Even with training, not all dogs will develop this special sense, and if they do, it usually only becomes apparent over time. But Quincy was able to sense Amber's seizures without training, and was able to do so right from the start.

For the next seven months Amber attended the Saturday morning training classes on a regular basis. During that time Quincy learned mobility assistance skills such as opening and closing doors, retrieving dropped items and providing balance and support for Amber when she walks.

Quincy is very intelligent, responding to both voice and hand signals, and his ability to detect oncoming seizures is nothing short of astonishing. Not only can Quincy sense Amber's seizures five to 10 minutes in advance, but he can tell what *kind* of seizure she is going to have, and has learned to alert her in very distinct ways. For complex partial seizures, Quincy will lick Amber's hand. For grand mal seizures he will jump onto her lap if she is sitting. If she is standing, he will position himself in front of her so she cannot move, letting her know that she needs to find a safe place to lie down.

Another skill that Quincy developed is called "seizure response." This includes anything a dog is trained to do after a seizure occurs, and can range from summoning help to providing comfort and support. In Quincy's case, he was trained to lie on top of Amber during a grand mal seizure, to prevent her from injuring herself. This skill needed to be refined; initially Quincy would lie across her legs but because she kicks, often violently, he now positions himself on her chest instead.

Quincy has made a remarkable difference in Amber's life. Her last two years of high school were not only bearable, they were fun. Students started approaching Amber and asking questions about her dog. "They thought he was *awesome*," she recalls. Quincy is also a great conversation starter. "I used to be really shy and withdrawn, but I can talk forever when it comes to my dog."

With renewed confidence, Amber joined several extracurricular clubs and the school newspaper. New medication helped to reduce her seizures from several times daily, to once or twice a week, and she no longer feared being alone and helpless when they occurred. She even started volunteering with the Future Farmers of America (FFA) club, tending chickens after school with only her canine "early warning system" for company.

In the rare event that Amber didn't heed Quincy's alerts, he would go the extra mile. One time, she was hurrying through the halls at school. It was crowded, the bell had just rung and she was late for class. Quincy made several attempts to alert Amber, but she was too preoccupied to notice. Finally, he very gently took her arm in his mouth, pulled her down to the ground, then sat on top of her so she couldn't move. Amber was grateful. Quincy had prevented a potentially serious, and embarrassing, fall.

Quincy was such an important part of Amber's success in high school that when it came time for graduation, she wanted to share the celebrations with him. As the class filed into the auditorium to receive their diplomas, Quincy walked beside Amber, dressed in his own cap and gown. He accompanied her onto the stage when the choir sang. Then, along with the rest of the class, Amber threw her cap – along with Quincy's – into the air.

"At the prom, Quincy was my date," Amber tells me. "I'm not the kind of girl most guys want to ask out, so I took Quincy. He even wore a bow tie." Throughout the evening, she sat at a table with friends while Quincy rested quietly at her feet. A couple of boys asked her to dance, and Quincy joined them so Amber could lean on him for support. "It was kind of funny," she recalls. "They weren't used to dancing with a dog."

Amber and Quincy (Photo: Joan Bussard)

As the celebrations wore down, it was time for the last dance of the night. Slow music started to play, and Quincy accompanied Amber onto the dance floor. It was just the two of them this time and they shared a dance to a Kenny Chesney tune. The song was called, quite fittingly, "Me and You."

Since high school, Amber has remained in Oxford. She walks as much as she can, but uses a wheelchair for long distances and for her daily "runs" with Quincy around the local track. She continues to teach Quincy new skills, building on the ones he already has, and he is only too happy to lend a helping "paw."

When talking with Amber, it's clear how much she loves the dog that she's nicknamed "Mr. Wiggles," because he is "so wiggly and happy and fun to be around." Amber is especially pleased that he is a rescued dog. "I think they give back a lot more; they appreciate you more. The way they look at you, it's as if they know that they are getting a second chance. I guess I'm biased, but they're the best kind of dog to love."

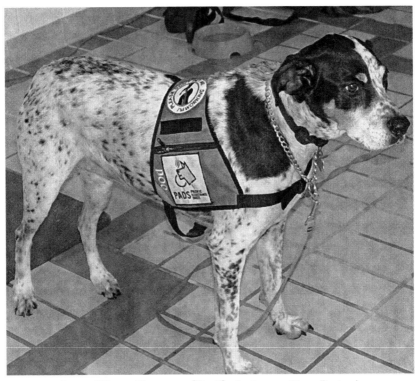

Beans (Photo: Courtesy of Pacific Assistance Dogs Society)

A Helping Ear

One afternoon, Jim Luettgen was lying on his couch taking a nap. All of a sudden Beans, his service dog, leaped full force on top of him. Jim awoke with a start. "It was a real BOOM!" he says. "You know how a toddler jumps up on you? It was kind of like that."

Jim has severe hearing loss, and Beans is trained to alert him to sounds like doorbells, oven timers, his special adaptive phone and alarms. Usually Beans "paws" at Jim to get his attention, and then leads him towards the sound. But this time it was different. As soon as Jim woke up, Beans immediately went down on the floor into a crouch position – the signal for "fire."

Jim was confused. He doesn't wear his hearing aid when he sleeps, because it is too uncomfortable, so he hadn't heard any alarm. But he couldn't smell any smoke either. Jim is usually a pretty affable guy, except when he's woken up in the middle of a nap. "What? Are you crazy?" he growled. "There's no fire! What in the world is going on?"

Beans was persistent, so Jim finally got up off the couch and took a look around. When he reached the kitchen, he stopped cold in his tracks. "Just beyond the doorway was the stove, and it was engulfed in fire. Flames were shooting up from it. They were three feet high!"

Jim had been simmering a soup bone on the stove when he fell asleep. The fat from the bone had bubbled over onto the burner and caught on fire. Jim managed to grab several boxes of baking soda and a couple of pot lids to put it out. But he got there just in the nick of time. "It was probably a minute or two away from the whole place going up," he says. "Beans saved me. I would have been dead; or covered with third-degree burns."

Jim has what is known as late onset bilateral sensorineural hearing loss, a genetic condition that occurs in adulthood. He was in his mid forties when he first began to experience problems. At the time he was living in Alberta and working as a forensic psychologist in a psychiatric hospital. Many of the patients at the hospital had committed extremely violent offences, including sexual assault and murder, but had been found not criminally responsible for their acts. Jim did assessments, ran therapy groups, and reported to judicial boards on patient progress. Since he was also trained to restrain aggressive patients, he was part of the critical emergency response team.

Over a period of nine months, Jim experienced a near-total hearing loss. At first he would miss out on snippets of conversation. "Hey Jim, are you deaf?" colleagues would joke when he asked them to repeat what was said. Soon he had trouble making out what patients were telling him. It got to the point that he had to double-check things with the social worker. For instance, he might ask, "Patient X told me he was innocent, that he didn't commit that offence. Did he tell you the same thing?"

Forensic psychiatry is a hearing-critical profession, and Jim struggled to find ways to compensate. He considered using a microphone, but that would have been nearly impossible given the level of background noise in the hospital. Nor would a microphone be feasible when working with patients who were even the least bit paranoid.

Things came to a head one afternoon when Jim was in the discharge unit. He suddenly realized that, except for himself, the normally busy area was completely empty. As it turned out, there had been a fire alarm. All the other staff members had cleared out. "Management was not happy that I did not respond," he says. "An assessment of my hearing was conducted in my various roles and it was determined that my hearing was just not good enough." Jim could have fought the assessment, but decided against it. "I told them to put me out to pasture," he chuckles. Still, it was clearly painful for him. "I went from respected professional to rehab."

"Rehab" was the Island Deaf & Hard of Hearing Centre (ID-HHC) in Victoria, a city located on the southern tip of Vancouver Island. Jim had always wanted to move to the west coast, and settled into a small basement suite on the outskirts of town. For the next two years, he participated in several community-based programs at the Centre, which provides counseling and social services for those dealing with hearing loss. He learned lip-reading and American Sign Language (ASL), the predominant language used by the deaf community in North America. He also practiced various coping strategies, such as having people sit where there was light on their face, asking them to repeat things by saying them in a different way, and having them spell words that are difficult to understand. He also began looking for work, because he felt he was too young to retire.

Jim knew searching for a job would be difficult, but he faced an unanticipated problem. He would send out resumés, be called for a job interview, and then sleep through the alarm. Alarm clocks designed for the hard of hearing have flashing lights and pulsate, but "I can sleep through earthquakes," Jim says. He tried a vibrating bed, one advertised to wake even the heaviest sleepers, but that didn't work. "Vibrations only make me sleep more." In desperation Jim tried staying awake all night when he had an interview the next morning, which left him exhausted, frustrated and not in peak form.

Jim faced another challenge as well. Gregarious and outgoing, with a deep throaty laugh, he had always been popular, the life-of-the-party. Now, he had trouble making friends. "Hearing loss can be socially isolating," Jim reveals. "Typically, when you're in a new town and you want to meet people, you go to a dance or a bar." But background music and noise made it impossible to hear what people were saying, or to carry on a conversation. Coffee shops and restaurants were the same. "People think I'm stuck up. Either that, or they think I'm just ignoring them."

Despite the coping strategies he had learned, Jim found it diffi-cult to adjust to a world without sound. As a result he became with-drawn, if not clinically depressed. So, when an audiologist told Jim about hearing dogs and the work they do, he was eager to investigate.

Jim contacted Pacific Assistance Dogs Society (PADS), a non-profit organization that serves the western Canadian provinces of British Columbia, Alberta, Saskatchewan and Manitoba. PADS doesn't have a wait list per se, although it usually takes a significant amount of time to find an appropriate client/dog match. Jim submit-ted an application – and a couple of months later he was contacted about Beans. That was an unusually short time to wait. But then Beans' situation was unusual, too.

Beans, a black-and-white terrier mix, was just a few weeks old when she was found running loose in a trailer park, in a small town in northern British Columbia. It was mid-November, the temperatures were below freezing, and she was very ill. Esther Pedersen, a volunteer with the local SPCA, was at the shelter the day Beans was brought in. Ester recalls seeing her for the first time. "She was so small at the time, the skinniest dog I'd ever seen, with this enormous belly pro-truding between her legs." But she was definitely plucky. "She had this amazing spirit, despite her condition." Esther decided to take the little pup home and foster her.

Esther bought the highest quality puppy food she could find. With proper nutrition and caring, the little dog underwent a growth spurt. However, puppy food is very high in protein and calcium, so her bones grew quickly while her muscles and tendons were unable to keep pace. Her joints would not extend fully, and when she walked, her gait was awkward and wobbly, reminding Esther of the comical character created by British actor Rowan Atkinson: Mr. Bean. And that's how the little dog got her name.

A vet suggested switching to adult food, which slowed down the rate of growth in Bean's bones, and as the pup grew stronger Esther began to think about what the future might hold. Although she had volunteered with the shelter for three years, and had been involved in fostering and adopting over 350 dogs, Esther felt a special affinity for Beans. The dog was very clever, gentle and even-tempered. "She always looked boldly, with this intelligent keenness, straight at your eyes." Esther was familiar with PADS, having successfully placed one dog with them, and felt Beans would be a perfect fit. Soon Beans was on a plane bound for Vancouver to begin her new career as a service dog.

Beans spent eight months with puppy raisers who introduced her to all sorts of different social situations, and taught her basic commands. And even though the little pup no longer limped, she continued to live up to her name because she was always energetic and "full of beans!" The little dog loved racing around the yard, playing fetch, and "showing off" some of her more unusual talents, such as "skating" on frozen surfaces, or sticking her head in a bucket of water and blowing bubbles through her nose.

When Beans was a year old, she went to PADS for advanced training. Since she was very social and comfortable around wheelchairs, it was originally thought she would make a good mobility assistance dog. But that idea didn't pan out! Beans has an independent streak, and once she'd learned to open and close doors, she started to come and go as she pleased. She would let herself into the training room, get some toys out of a drawer, and take them outside to play. One time she opened all the kennel doors, letting the other dogs into the exercise yard as well. Perhaps this made Beans popular with her canine pals, but a person with a mobility impairment would be hard-pressed to manage such a free-roaming dog.

Ron Tymrick, Beans' trainer, devised Plan B. "I decided to give her a whirl and see if she would make a good hearing dog," he says. The first step was to assess Beans' level of aptitude for the role. This involved setting a digital oven timer, then bringing her into a room where there were several people, lots of distractions and a variety of treats.

"Lots of dogs just ignore the timer when it goes off," Ron says. But not Beans. Her ears pricked up and she looked around for the source of the sound. Then, of her own accord, she went to check it out. That was the reaction Ron was hoping for. "Aptitude and willingness are the only things I can't teach a dog. I can mold them, I can shape them and bring them to the forefront, but they have to be there from the start."

Like all PADS hearing dogs, Beans' initial training was done using a clicker, a small, hand-held device about the size of a matchbox. Two or three people, with pockets full of treats, take turns "clicking" the device; the dog must determine where the sound is coming from, then approach the correct person and make contact. It is crucial that the dog make contact, since this is the way that hearing dogs alert their owners to sounds.

The next stage involves having the people holding the clickers play hide-and-seek. Ron explains the reason for this. "You aren't usually standing in the middle of a room when your phone goes off. The dog has to find you, sometimes even digging under covers to wake you up." After mastering that, a remote control device similar to a garage door opener is used to create sounds in other areas of the building; the dog learns to touch the trainer and lead them to the sound.

The dog is then matched with a hearing-impaired person, and the two train together at PADS for several days. Ron, unseen by the dog, watches through a window from another room. This serves two purposes: since the client is the only one in the room, the dog is not confused as to who it should alert; and having Ron out of sight helps to transfer the dog's loyalty to the new owner.

Ron then spends several days at the client's house, familiarizing the dog with the unique sounds of their new environment and easing the transition period. After that, the client reports back to PADS every week for a period of three months, so that Ron can monitor progress and provide support should problems arise.

Beans graduated from the hearing dog program with flying colors, and was initially paired with a man who was very shy. But hearing dogs attract a lot of attention, and people were constantly stopping the gentleman to ask questions, often on streets or in busy stores where there is a lot of background noise. He did not like the social interaction and became increasingly frustrated. Three months later he returned Beans to PADS.

As Beans continued to grow, her size became an issue. Hearing dogs are usually small, since they alert their owners by jumping up on them. But Beans kept growing and soon tipped the scales at a whopping 50 pounds.

It was time for Plan C. "Perhaps," Ron thought, "she would make a good companion dog." Beans was placed with a woman with agoraphobia who was afraid to leave her home. This was not a good match, because Beans was too energetic and high-spirited to be cooped up all day. So once again, she found herself unemployed.

Ron was running out of ideas. Then, as fate would have it, Jim's application arrived at PADS. The trainers were cautiously optimistic. Beans clearly had talent as a hearing dog, and because Jim's a big guy, six feet tall and weighing 225 pounds, her size wouldn't be a problem for him. Ron felt it was "now or never" time. Beans was already three years old, and she deserved a permanent home. If things didn't work out this time, she would have to be placed as a family pet.

A meeting was arranged between Jim and Beans. Luckily, it couldn't have been a better match. "Right from the start, they seemed to click," Ron says. "You get pretty good at reading body language in my job, whether it's human or canine. Both of them just warmed up to each other. And the look on Jim's face when I brought the dog in, well, it was like, 'Wow. I can do this.'"

Jim and Beans (Photo: Niels Nohr)

The training went off without a hitch, and Beans soon became Jim's hearing service dog. But it wasn't clear sailing for her just yet! She was so enthusiastic about her new job that she would alert Jim by jumping up on him full throttle, at about 25 miles per hour, tackling him in the groin! So it was back to PADS for more training, where Beans learned to alert by gently tapping Jim's leg with her paw.

These days Jim works as a civil servant in child and family development. He is very active, swimming several times a week and playing underwater hockey, and has a close circle of friends. And the skinny little dog from the trailer park has finally found her niche. Beans goes everywhere with Jim, even hanging out on the deck of the pool while he swims. She is ever vigilant, carefully screening sounds, deciding what is useful and what is background noise.

Hearing loss is an invisible disability; one that is not immediately apparent. Since Jim's loss occurred as an adult, he speaks clearly, and strangers assume he can hear. He recalls a business trip he took without Beans, where he had to change planes in Houston. "It was just after 9/11 and the airport security had enforced the 'take off your shoes' procedure," he says. Jim didn't hear them and just walked through the line. "Six really big Texas security guards were on my back before I knew what hit me. If Beans had been with me, folks would have realized that she was a hearing dog. One important thing assistance dogs do is let other people know there is something different about you."

Still, a lot of what Beans does is less intangible. She provides a "hearing window" to the world. While walking down a street, when Beans turns around, Jim will realize someone is coming up behind him. On a stroll through the park, if she stops to look at something, Jim will follow her gaze and see a bird in a tree, or a child at play. And as for staying up all night, fearing he will sleep through the alarm: there is no longer any need. Beans wakes him up without fail. "She gets her breakfast in the morning right after I get up. There's no way she's going to let me sleep in."

Beans is Jim's lifesaver, helper and friend. "I consider myself a very lucky guy." After Beans alerted Jim to the kitchen fire, he called PADS to let them know she had saved his life. They were relieved that Jim was okay and excited for Beans. "After all the time and effort, all the trials and tribulations and everything she's gone through, to have Beans do something that was so outstanding, it really makes my job worthwhile," Ron says. "It's that extra 'paycheck' for me, knowing she has achieved something that not many dogs achieve."

The Miracle of Children and Dogs

In 1987, Karen Shirk was studying towards a degree in social work. A typical college student, she ate junk food, partied a lot and pulled all-nighters cramming for exams. Karen was always tired but then again, so were all her friends. She chalked it up to normal student pressures. That is, until she suffered respiratory arrest.

Karen was diagnosed with myasthenia gravis, a rare neuromuscular disease that causes progressive paralysis. The muscles surrounding her lungs were also affected and she needed to use a ventilator at night to help her breathe. All of a sudden Karen's carefree, spirited college days were replaced by long hospital stays. The situation was made even more lonely and depressing when all but her closest friends seemed to disappear.

Karen felt a service dog would help her regain a certain level of independence, but when she applied to several organizations, much to her dismay, she was turned away. Karen was "too disabled," she was told. They only placed dogs with applicants who could be reintegrated back into the community, which they felt was not a realistic expectation in her case.

When one organization agreed to place Karen on their waiting list, she was elated. They called 18 months later to say they had found the perfect match, and sent a trainer to visit in order to determine what skills the dog would need. But Karen's hopes were quickly dashed. She received a follow-up letter in the mail stating, "We're sorry, we don't place dogs with people who are on ventilators."

Fortunately for Karen, she had a friend who refused to let her wallow in despair. Instead, she insisted that Karen adopt her own dog and train it herself. And that's how Karen came to meet a black, 30-pound bundle of fur that she named "Ben, My Courage and Friend." The two quickly became inseparable. They attended obedience classes and Karen enlisted the help of a local trainer to teach Ben the skills he needed to be able to help around the house.

Then one night Karen returned home from the hospital after having open-heart surgery. She had been given a morphine pump to help ease the pain. The morphine, combined with Karen's other medication, proved to be potentially lethal. She lost consciousness and was literally fighting for her life when the telephone rang.

Ben picked up the phone and laid it beside Karen, as he'd been trained to do. When she didn't respond, he started barking frantically into the receiver. Karen's father, who was on the other end of the line, realized something was wrong and called for an ambulance. If not for Ben's intervention, Karen would have almost certainly died.

That autumn, Karen and Ben were sitting in the field behind their house watching the colorful leaves fall from the trees. Karen reminisced about all the gifts that Ben had brought into her life and wondered how many other people were in need of the same sort of miracle. She imagined an organization where anyone who wanted and needed a service dog, would be able to get one; where nobody would be turned away. And that's how 4 Paws for Ability, Inc. was born.

Ben was not only the inspiration for Karen's dream, he was an integral part of it becoming a reality. He was there through the planning stages; he was at the first board meeting. And he was there when Karen told a 12-year-old girl – paralyzed from a spinal stroke and turned down by other organizations – that she would be getting a service dog.

While many organizations will not place service dogs with children, over ninety-five percent of the dogs that 4 Paws for Ability places are with those under the age of 12. True to Karen's ideal of providing service dogs to as many individuals as possible, the organization does not discriminate based on age, type or severity of disability, or economic status. As long as a client (or their parent/guardian) is able to take care of a dog, they have a letter from a physician, and are considered disabled under the Americans with Disabilities Act, they are eligible to apply.

Another goal of the organization is to assist with animal rescue by obtaining as many dogs as possible from shelters and rescue groups. And because they serve a wide variety of clients, they don't necessarily need "retrieving" dogs, so many are mutts and smaller dogs that don't look anything like the conventional service dog. But they all have one thing in common: a very big heart.

Noah and Harry

The most frequent request "4 Paws" receives is for autism service dogs. Autism is a neurological disorder that begins in early childhood and is usually diagnosed before the age of three. Autistic children have difficulty with both verbal and non-verbal communication, and with social interactions. They often have repetitive behaviors that range from harmless ones, such as hand flapping or rocking, to more severe behavior such as head banging. Another common trait is that they need a structured, routine environment in order to feel safe.

4 Paws for Ability was the first agency in the United States to place skilled autism service dogs, and continues to be the largest organization to do so. Karen has a deep understanding of the disorder and how it affects each child differently. She stresses the importance of creating a three-point team that consists of the dog, the child and the parent(s).

It was this special understanding of autism that attracted Cathy and Kelley Foust of St. Peters, Missouri, to 4 Paws for Ability when they were looking for a service dog for their son. Noah is 10 years old, with extremely poor communication skills. He has trouble processing sounds, including words that are being spoken to him. His speech is limited and unclear, making it difficult for even his parents to understand, and he has used sign language since he was four years old. Noah is also very quick to experience anger, frustration and aggression; he will lash out by pinching and kicking others, slamming doors and even hitting himself.

Perhaps one of the most alarming aspects of Noah's autism is what is known as "elopement." He has no concept of danger, is very fast and can take off at any moment. This is a common tendency in children with autism. Their parents sometimes refer to them as "little Houdinis," because they can escape from even the most secure situations. This was a constant concern for Cathy and Kelley. They installed locks on all the windows, keypad locks on the doors, and alarms and double fences in the backyard. Still, Noah manages to escape, working any lock and tackling any barrier that stands in his way.

Cathy says it was terrifying to suddenly turn around and realize that Noah had taken off and to have absolutely no idea where, or even in which direction, he had gone. Twice, passing motorists have stopped to rescue him as he raced through the streets. Although he wasn't far from home, because he was unable to communicate where he lived, the police had to be called.

As for going out in public, "It was ugly," Cathy says. She tried everything she could think of to keep her son safe and contained. Noah hated holding hands with an adult and would have a "meltdown," yelling and screaming, whenever she insisted. He was too big to fit into a stroller or a grocery cart. Cathy even tried a special wheelchair, but Noah managed to get out of it and race across the mall. Bystanders looked on in amazement, probably wondering why on earth anyone would confine a child to a wheelchair when he was perfectly mobile.

When Noah started school, it was stressful not only for him, but for everyone else involved. Noah attends special classes for part of the day, and having to move between different classrooms made him nervous. His teachers were challenged by Noah's 15 to 20 daily attempts to bolt out the door, and two staff members with walkie-talkies were needed to keep track of him when he was outside in the schoolyard.

By the time Noah was in grade two, his exhausted parents decided to look into getting him an autism service dog. They already had a sweet tri-colored Australian shepherd named Bounce, but realized that Noah needed something more. "We didn't just want a well-trained dog," Cathy says. "We wanted one that could handle Noah on a daily basis."

When the Fousts contacted 4 Paws for Ability, they learned that the average cost of a service dog was around $10,000. However, they were encouraged by the organization's fundraising approach. The organization partners with clients to help raise the funds, so that dogs can be made available as quickly as possible, often in less than 10 months time.

Prospective clients raise money in a variety of ways, such as approaching local groups for donations, holding garage sales and selling raffle tickets. One enterprising woman even baked dog cookies and sold them in the local parks.

Cathy realized that she would have to think creatively if she was to be successful. She held a "trivia night" at the Knights of Columbus hall, selling tickets, making appetizers and providing beverages for the event. She also approached Vista Grande, a popular local Mexican restaurant that agreed to donate 20 percent of one night's profit to help Noah's cause.

Once the Fousts had raised the funds, they made a video of Noah and sent it to 4 Paws so that a dog could be trained specifically to meet his unique physical and emotional needs. Noah was paired with

Harry, a young, black Labrador retriever who had been rescued from the humane society when he was four months old. Harry has a laid-back personality and strong work drive, which makes him a natural for this type of job. As Cathy put it, "They couldn't have found a more perfect match."

Noah and his parents traveled to Ohio to take part in an intensive ten-day training session, along with his brother Spencer, who was ten-years-old at the time. The organization encourages siblings to attend the training because it gives them an opportunity to become involved. For Spencer, it was the "best vacation ever;" trainer Jeremy Dulebohn let him help with the care of the dogs and assist in demonstrating some of the commands.

During the training session, the Fousts and Harry worked on skills that would help Noah in his daily life. For instance, one important skill for autism service dogs is being able to help a child deal with sensory overload. Noah, like many autistic children, is hypersensitive to sights, sounds, smells and touch. He is often unable to discern which information is important and which is background "noise." An alarm, for example, may seem no more important to Noah than the sound of a bird, the smell of flowers, or the touch of the sun on his arms. Autism service dogs alert to important sounds, and also provide focus and a sense of calm should a child become over stimulated.

One unique aspect of 4 Paws is that their autism service dogs are trained in tracking, an important skill when working with children like Noah. Should a child manage to escape, the dogs are trained to track them down by scent, even if they have been missing for quite some time. Harry proved his mettle at tracking right from the start. During practice sessions, Noah wandered away twice and much to Cathy and Kelley's relief, he was quickly found.

Another important skill is "tethering." When out in public, Noah and Harry both wear a special harness and are tethered together by a leash. If Noah makes a sudden move or starts to bolt, Harry is trained to brace. He will crouch low to the ground and "dig in his heels" to prevent Noah from running away. Tethering has had a life-changing effect on the Fousts. "Harry has given us back the freedom to take Noah places without the fear of losing him or suffering countless tantrums," Cathy says.

Children with autism often form a closer bond with animals than they do with members of their immediate family. In Noah's case this bond didn't occur right away. Harry had different fur and a different smell than his Australian shepherd at home, and Noah had difficulty adapting to the change. Upon meeting Harry, Noah petted him and then smelled his hand, then declared that this was "not my dog."

Noah also saw Harry as an authority figure; one who wasn't going to let him go wherever he wanted, or do whatever he pleased. It took about six months for Noah to bond with Harry, until he realized the Lab was not "all work and no play." In fact, much of the time he's just a big, goofy dog who took over the leather recliner in the living room from the very first day.

These days, Noah and Harry go everywhere together. They share love and kisses on a daily basis. Noah would even like Harry to get into the bathtub with him – but since Harry is probably the only Lab on the planet who doesn't like water, he sits on the bath mat instead.

Harry is always on duty, keeping Noah safe. At home, if Noah starts to head outside on his own or he begins fiddling with a lock, Harry will bark, whine and run in circles to attract Cathy or Kelley's attention. And last summer, Harry went one step further. The family was at a lake when Noah suddenly jumped a fence, raced towards the water and headed straight in. Harry was not very far behind, and despite the fact that he hates water, he dove in and circled around in front of Noah, preventing him from going out any further. He held his position firmly, until several adults reached the lake and pulled Noah out.

At school, Harry has his own ID badge and his photo is on the staff poster in the hall. Noah is calmer and better behaved, with fewer outbursts and no more attempts to escape. During recess, a teacher's

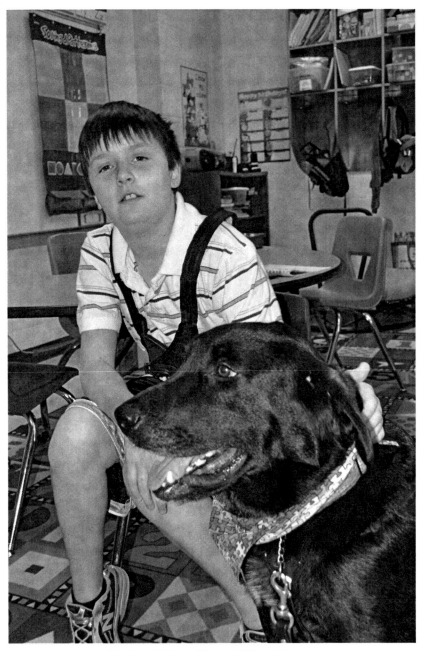

Noah and Harry (Photo: Tiffany Fowler)

assistant simply holds onto Harry's leash, and both of them keep a watchful eye on Noah as he enjoys his playtime.

With Harry's companionship, Noah interacts more with his peers and has become more active and socially involved. He plays on a special baseball team, something that would have been impossible before. When Noah hits the ball, he runs around the bases while tethered to Harry. Then, when it's Noah's turn in the outfield, the other players often stop to pet Harry as they make their way between first and second base.

He is regularly invited to birthday parties and he brings home numerous drawings and notes from his classmates. This social aspect wasn't something that the Fousts expected to happen when they thought about getting a service dog, but as Cathy says, "It is certainly 'icing on the cake.'"

These days, Cathy can't imagine life without Harry. "He gives us peace of mind, which we never thought was possible. He is extremely gentle, patient, tolerant, intelligent and loyal, with a tail that never stops wagging."

Lily and Grizwald

Harry is just one of the many success stories at 4 Paws for Ability. Grizwald, a multi-purpose service dog, is another. Multi-purpose service dogs are taught skills that are "tailor made" to the unique needs of each child. "Many of the families come to 4 Paws asking if we can help their child who may have a disability not addressed by any of the service dog agencies they have located," Karen Shirk explains.

Grizwald is partnered with Lily, a young girl who was adopted from an orphanage in China when she was 16 months old. "Grizwald is a godsend to us," Lily's mother, Nancy, says. "He is an angel with four paws, a buddy to everyone in our family and a clown all rolled into one amazing dog. He's 50 pounds of fluff and love, and does what no human being can do for our severely traumatized daughter."

Nancy, a former special education teacher, was working as the executive director for a non-profit organization at the time of the adoption. Her husband, David, taught high school social studies, and their beautiful daughter Zoe was five years old. When Nancy and David decided to adopt a child from China, they prepared themselves by taking classes and by learning about the country's culture, government and politics. They knew that Chinese orphanages can be overcrowded and that the children are often subjected to trauma, neglect and even abuse.

But when they traveled to China, they were still unprepared for the horrific conditions they found. Lily was in a state-run orphanage, which apparently housed mental patients as well. The institution was massively overcrowded and understaffed, with a child/caregiver ratio of 25:1. The couple was not allowed inside the orphanage. Instead, they were shown to a "holding room" which Nancy describes as "Sterile, clean-tiled and eerily silent. There wasn't a toy in sight."

Nancy and David were told that Lily had been abandoned in front of a women's hospital shortly after her birth. She was catatonic at the time, and had remained so for several days. During her stay at the orphanage, it was clear that the child had been severely neglected and abused. There were unexplained marks and scars on her body, and she also suffered from severe, chronic acid reflux that had caused a painful ulcer in her esophagus.

Even now, after eight years of constant love and support, Lily still suffers from the effects of her pre-adoptive abuse. Except for the few spontaneous words uttered in her sleep, she is mute. She is fearful of dolls and is uncomfortable around small children; her trauma team suspects that this may stem from being punished by being placed in a room along with very sick and dying children.

Lily also experiences dissociative episodes and flashbacks. While in the depths of a flashback, she kicks, screams and claws in terror. "We often walk a tightrope because you never know what might trigger an episode," Nancy says. "The responses to trauma triggers are not behaviors in the traditional sense. You can't shape them. Trauma changes the chemistry of a child's developing brain and the triggered episodes become autonomic responses. The child becomes stuck in fight, flight or freeze mode."

Nancy and David have tried countless therapies and interventions, but the best medicine by far has been Grizwald, a scruffy terrier cross who was rescued from a shelter when he was only a few months old. Grizwald has been trained to give Lily comfort and support, calming her in times of trauma and stress with a touch or a kiss. *Lap* is his cue to rest his head on her knee; *paws up*, and he gently puts his paws on her chair. At night, he nestles beside Lily and applies deep pressure with his body to help her relax and fall asleep.

Grizwald's very presence keeps Lily centered and stable. In the two years they have been together, her flashbacks have decreased dramatically. They used to occur three or four times a day, lasting up to four and a half hours. Now she experiences about one a month and it lasts less than 15 minutes.

Grizwald also gives Lily confidence when the family goes out in public, something they were unable to do before he came along. In malls and in other crowded areas – even at Disney World – he acts like a security blanket, grounding Lily and helping her to feel safe. In restaurants he sits under the table, and Lily will often take off her shoes and rest her feet gently on his back. And when Zoe, who is now 13, wanted to attend a Jonas Brothers concert, the entire family went along. Grizwald wore headphones to block out the sound, prompting numerous comments about how he was a very "cool" dog.

Nancy and David are grateful to have two such amazing daughters. At the time of Lily's adoption, they truly believed that the child they were matched with would be the child they were meant to parent. That belief has been reinforced many times since. Although it is often difficult, they feel truly blessed. "Someone upstairs obviously thinks we have the ability to do this," Nancy says. And as for Grizwald, "He has a healing impact on our entire family. To think this furry four-legged critter could turn our household from upside down to right side up in such a short period of time is nothing short of miraculous."

Lily and Grizwald (Photo: Ellen Petersen)

Success stories like these are what Karen was hoping for when she created 4 Paws for Ability. They are what keeps her motivated as she continues her life's work; training dogs and placing them with those in need. To date, she has placed over 300 dogs.

"When I think about how close I came to death, I now celebrate every minute that I am alive," Karen says. "I still have myasthenia gravis. It has robbed me of many physical abilities, but in many ways, it has actually strengthened my life. Without it, I would not have had Ben and I would not be where I am today. Because of this amazing dog, I regained my zest for life and now live the most rewarding life I could ever dream of."

Karen is mother to four adopted children: Aaron from Bulgaria, and Elijah, Isaiah and Isabelle who are biological siblings from Haiti. And they are clearly aware of the role Ben played in her life. Recently, Aaron solemnly told her, "I'm glad Ben saved your life. If he hadn't, I would not have a mom. Well, I might have had another mom come to get me, but they wouldn't have been a mom *like you.*"

Rover Rehab

Nova is not your typical prison inmate. Skinny, cheerful and with an abundance of energy, he runs around in circles searching for a wayward treat that has fallen on the floor. He finds it, gobbles it up, then jumps up on the bed and gives his cellmate a big, sloppy kiss. Nova doesn't know how long he's been in prison, nor does he know when he's getting parole. It could be days, weeks, or even months; but he doesn't mind. There is good food and plenty of love here. Oh… and a friend to scratch those places that are ever so hard to reach.

Nova is one of the dogs who are part of "Rover Rehab." Life is very different from when he was a stray wandering the streets. He is now being trained by inmates at the Warren Correctional Institution in Lebanon, Ohio. Soon he will have a new purpose and a new life: helping an autistic child, or one with a physical disability, perhaps.

The idea of having prison inmates train dogs was the brainchild of Sister Pauline Quinn, a Dominican nun. She first placed shelter dogs at the Washington Correctional Center for Women in Gig Harbor, Washington, in 1981. The Prison Pet Partnership Program®, as it came to be known, was incorporated in 1991, and more than 700 dogs have been trained as service dogs and partnered with those with disabilities.

Since then, several other prison pet programs have been created. Some take severely traumatized dogs – those considered "unadoptable" by most standards – and rehabilitate them so they can be adopted out as family pets. Others train breeder-donated dogs to either become service dogs, or to work as explosive detection canines and police dogs. Although the specific focus of these programs may vary, they all recognize the powerful bond that can form between humans and animals. When inmates work with animals, they not only gain valuable skills, but increased compassion, confidence and the sense of fulfillment that comes from knowing they are making a positive contribution to the lives of others.

The Warren Correctional Institution is one of three facilities that partners with 4 Paws for Ability to train service dogs. The inmates raise puppies, socialize them, and help teach them basic obedience as well as specialized skills. Grizwald and Harry, the dogs mentioned in "The Miracle of Children and Dogs," are both former Rover Rehab dogs.

4 Paws for Ability founder Karen Shirk feels that the inmates and rescued dogs share many important characteristics. "They both understand rejection, abandonment, sadness and despair. They have found themselves outcasts from society and looking at the world through the bars of a locked, closed door," she states. "Many times, the inmates have had little or no experience with unconditional love or forgiveness. They have not felt the joy that can be experienced from doing something that will deeply affect another's life. The light that returns to the eyes of both the inmates and the dogs is an amazing thing to see. It's the miracle of healing."

Regina Szente agrees. Regina is the institution coordinator at the Warren Correctional Center, and is in charge of the day-to-day running of the Prison Pet Partnership Program. "It's amazing to watch the inmates with the dogs," she says. "They are very patient when it comes to training them. Some of the inmates are doing a life sentence and will never get out of prison. This program offers them a chance to do something great for the community and gives them a sense of purpose."

Regina explains that the dogs are selected from local shelters and brought to the center by the staff of 4 Paws. They live in the prison, sharing a cell with two inmates: a primary handler who is responsible for the majority of the dog's care, feeding and grooming; and a secondary handler who provides backup if the primary handler is ill or unavailable. In that way someone is with the dogs at all times.

In order to participate in the program, the inmates undergo a rigorous screening process. Among other things, they must not have had any gang affiliation, history of domestic or animal abuse, and not have had a Rules Infraction Board (RIB) ticket within the last year.

Every Monday afternoon Jeremy Dulebohn, the training director at 4 Paws, conducts a training session at the prison. He gives the group general instructions, then helps the inmates teach basic obedience skills. While the inmates practice, Jeremy walks around the room, offering suggestions and guidance. Often a dog's innate talents only become apparent over time, so he keeps a close eye on each dog's development to see what they are especially good at. He spends time talking with each of the inmates about their dog's progress, and encourages them to focus on particular skills, such as mobility or tracking.

"It must be 'brain-racking' for him, because there are so many people and so many dogs," says program participant Eddie Hill, referring to the fact that there can be up to 18 dogs in the program at any one time.

Hill was in prison for several years before he decided to become involved with the program. "I just ended up loving it," he says in a long, easy drawl. It is clear how appreciative Hill is of the dogs, and the difference they have made in his life. "You have something to take care of. You have to be responsible for the dog and gear your day around the dog's needs. It's nice to come back to your cell at the end of the day and somebody's there that likes you and is happy to see you."

Hill has kept a list of all the dogs he has worked with, and Nova is his 26th dog. Most of these go on to become mobility service dogs, and he has vast experience not only teaching basic commands, but skills needed for this type of work.

Eddie Hill (Photo: Karen Shirk)

Hill enthusiastically describes how he goes about training dogs for various tasks. For instance, one useful skill the dogs learn is turning a light on and off. "The first step is holding a treat above the switch on the wall," he explains. "When the dog comes to get the treat, they will accidentally bump the light switch with their nose. So you praise them up real good and give them the treat. The dogs are usually pretty quick to pick up on this. They think, 'Okay, when I bump my nose on the switch, I get love and a reward,' and they just start bumping it on their own. Pretty soon you can just be standing a ways back and when you say *light,* they'll jump up there and turn it on." Once a dog learns to turn on a light, turning it off is fairly easy. "If they go to turn a switch on and it's already up, they'll usually just kind of pull it down on their own."

Another skill Hill teaches is opening and closing doors. "First we get the dog to play tug, by gently pulling on a toy. Once they learn to pull it in an even manner, we tie a string or something around the doorknob, with the toy on the other end of it. When the dog pulls the toy, the door opens and it's the same thing, you praise them and give them a treat. Then you wean them off the toy, to where they are just pulling on something hanging on the doorknob."

Shutting a door begins with teaching a dog the command *touch.* "We start by getting them to touch our hand and give them a treat when they do. Then we train them to touch a specific point on an object somewhere." Once the dog masters the touch command, "We tell them *touch,* using an open door and when they push it, they get treats and love. Then they start pushing it harder and harder, eventually shutting it. Then you change the command from *touch* to *close*."

Nova is one of the dogs in the prison program who shows an affinity for tracking. Like Harry in the previous chapter, he will go on to become an autism service dog. Hill says that in teaching Nova this skill, "The main thing is getting him to know he's supposed to have his nose on the ground and be smelling for something." This is accomplished by having the dog stay and watch, while treats are placed on the ground at every step or two. Then the command *track* is given and when Nova goes and picks up the treats, "You praise him up and tell him how good he is." Once he has the concept down, the treats are gradually spaced further and further apart and in a more sporadic line. Dogs like Nova learn to associate the trainer's scent with the treats on the ground, and eventually they learn to track the trainer by scent alone.

Hill admits that he gets very attached to the dogs, and when their stint in Rover Rehab ends, he hates to see them go. "But one thing about this is you see them going away in good health. You know they're going to be helping somebody and that makes you feel good. It's so very rewarding, 'cause you're helping a person and saving a dog's life at the same time."

Hill was one of the inmates who worked with Grizwald, a dog who is fondly remembered by everyone at the prison. "He was a very, very cute dog," Regina says. "He was sharp-looking, a short little thing with wiry hair. He was just so unique. Everybody wanted to work with Grizwald. Everyone loved him – the staff, the inmates, *everyone*."

Although Hill and Grizwald only worked together for a short period of time, the dog made quite an impression on him. "He was just a baby. He was good; such a good dog. We went through some potty training accidents, 'cause he was just a baby, but he was a good little dog. I liked him, he was just so cute."

Hill didn't know what happened to Grizwald. When told about Lily and her family and the positive impact the dog has had on them, he is obviously touched. "That's great," he says. After a brief pause he quietly adds, "That is just so great."

Hill has made mistakes in the past, but he is making up for it, Karen says. "Eddie has been in our program since day one." And while not overlooking the things he did in the past, "He is a phenomenal person here. The saddest thing is that only our dogs will ever know what a great person he has become, since he is in prison for life. He looks like a librarian or a schoolteacher and is so gentle and meek in spirit. He is a very soft-spoken man who genuinely loves his dogs. I saw a picture of him that had been taken when he was convicted; he was just a kid. Some guys never grow up or better themselves in prison. Eddie certainly has. He is a good man. I have been working with him for about eight years and I have a lot of respect for him."

Karen draws a parallel between the inmates and those with disabilities. "When it comes right down to it, many people with disabilities live in a prison as well," she says. Karen knows this only too well, as a result of her own disability. The walls may be invisible, but they are there, nonetheless. "The dogs bring a sense of fulfillment and self-esteem to the inmates, and then go out and bring the same to their new life partners. So much from a dog that somebody threw away."

Giving Life Balance

Amy first met Tucker at the San Francisco SPCA when he was 11 months old. She was hoping to find an active dog – one that would play catch – and this bouncy terrier cross seemed to be the perfect fit. He was extremely excited and full of energy. He chased a ball and raced around in circles. Then came the clincher: Tucker ran up, put his head between Amy's knees and did a somersault. "He made me laugh hysterically," Amy says.

Amy's laugh is infectious. A freelance Spanish interpreter, she has that kind of open frankness and good humor that you would want in a best friend. She lives in a small studio apartment in San Francisco, and loves going to movies and trying out new restaurants.

At first it is hard to imagine why someone like Amy would need a service dog. Yet, like millions of others, she suffers from an "invisible disability." Amy has bipolar disorder, which causes her moods to fluctuate. She cycles through periods of mania and depression, interspersed by "normal" moods.

When Amy is in her manic phase, she's in a state of "high flying euphoria," as she describes it. "You're on top of the world; you can do no wrong. You feel beautiful and invincible. No one has ever thought of anything as amazing as you're thinking right now." But these feelings are also accompanied by poor judgment and a lack of impulse control, such as making spur-of-the-moment purchases she can ill afford.

Then Amy crashes into a deep depression. She lacks energy and just wants to stay in bed. Even the routine activities of day-to-day living seem overwhelming; it is difficult to shower or dress, and impossible to work. These periods are devastating for Amy. "It feels like things will never get any better; like this is a permanent state that is never going to end."

Things that help alleviate her symptoms are exercise, sunshine and having a structured and consistent routine. But it's hard for her to do these things, especially during her depressive phase, when she needs them the most.

Amy has always loved animals, and for a long time she wanted to get a dog of her own, but the timing was never right. It certainly wasn't feasible during university – even though, while home on a summer vacation, she was tempted to take Sally, the family rottweiler, back to school with her. "Sally kept getting into the back of the truck while I was packing it to leave. Every time I came back with a load, she'd be lying down in the truck, curled up next to a box," Amy says. It was a difficult parting for them both. "I had to keep asking her to get out, and it broke my heart."

After graduation, getting a dog didn't seem to be a viable option, either. Amy began working sixty-hour weeks to establish her career. Then she moved to San Francisco for a new job, and with barely three days to find an apartment, she had to settle on one that, like most in the city, had a "no pets" policy.

As time passed, Amy's disability began to disrupt her life more and more. And as her symptoms deepened, so did her yearning for a dog. She strongly felt a dog would provide companionship, reduce the stress that often triggers her symptoms, and motivate her to "get up off the couch" and do errands, even on those days when she was going through her darkest, most depressive moods. "I soon realized I not only *wanted* a dog, I *needed* one," she says. "It was something I just had to do."

Amy spent hours researching on the Internet. She learned that the Americans with Disabilities Act defines disability as any "mental or physical condition which substantially limits a major life activity." A service dog is defined as one that is "individually trained to do work or perform tasks for the benefit of a person with a disability."

She also learned that the support service dogs provide is not limited to those with physical disabilities. Psychiatric service dogs are trained to assist those with a number of conditions, such as post-traumatic stress disorder, panic attacks, agoraphobia and depression. These dogs are granted the same rights as other service dogs, including public access in places like stores and restaurants. This meant that Amy, as a person with a legal disability, had the right to have a dog in her home, regardless of the "no pets" policy; and to train it to become her service dog. With this barrier out of the way, she began to search for the perfect dog.

Amy hoped to get a dog from Guide Dogs for the Blind, Inc. Some of their dogs don't graduate from the program for one reason or another – such as minor health issues or being afraid of loud noises – and are released for adoption to the public. She thought this situation would be ideal, since the dog would already be well-trained and could easily adapt to meet her needs. However, when she applied, she discovered there was a four-year waiting list. So Amy decided to rescue a dog from the SPCA and train it herself. That is how she ended up playing ball with Tucker that day.

If Amy had been able to find someone who knew about service animals to accompany her to the shelter, she would have chosen a more sedate dog. "Tucker was the worst dog I could have adopted *and* the best dog I could have adopted," she says. "I didn't know what I was getting into." Tucker is not what you'd call an "easy" dog. He is boisterous, with a strong prey drive, and wants to run after anything that moves. He is bright, curious and always trying to outfox Amy when it comes to obeying commands.

As for wanting a dog that would play catch: once they got home, Tucker was no longer interested. "It was bait and switch," Amy declares. It took him a year to get around to fetching a ball. "And even now, he still only brings it back when there is nothing more interesting to do."

Amy knew very little about training dogs. When she was growing up, her family had pets, but they were outside all day. Having a dog in a city with lots of people, a myriad of distractions and no backyard was a completely different matter.

Amy took Tucker to obedience classes and one-on-one lessons, but nothing worked. "Well, to be fair, it's not that nothing worked," Amy says. "He learned a lot and so did I, but there was just so *much* of him and I had to be on my toes at all times. Tucker reacted to everything and everybody. Taking a walk was a highly stressful venture, which is ironic considering what I wanted him for."

Amy was going through a difficult time in her personal life, as well. Bipolar symptoms are unpredictable, and she experienced a period of intense, boiling rage unlike anything she'd ever known before. She was totally unprepared for how to deal with this. That, plus the fact that Tucker was difficult to manage, made her life feel totally out of control.

Once again, Amy started searching the Internet. She came across a website for Discovery Dogs, an organization in the San Francisco Bay area that helps owners with disabilities train their own pets to be service dogs. Founder Shari Dehouwer realized that conventional dog obedience classes are not geared to people with disabilities. She developed a two-year program that provides more teaching time and support, as well as practice sessions that involve going into public places with a service dog.

Amy desperately wanted to work with Shari. She filled out an application form and went for an interview. Then Shari also met Tucker. "She probably took one look at Tucker and thought to herself, 'There's no way on God's green earth that this dog is going to be able to get public access because he is so energetic and easily distracted,'" Amy recalls.

That might be a bit of an exaggeration. Still, Shari knew that Tucker was a difficult dog. She also knew how much training him meant to Amy. So even though Shari works primarily with mobility assistance dogs, she agreed to work with Amy and Tucker.

Since training was not scheduled to start for a month, Shari gave Amy step-by-step instructions for things to work on with Tucker in the meantime. Amy practiced diligently, reminding herself to relax and take a deep breath whenever she felt frustrated or angry. Although it took superhuman effort to control her emotions, it was important to do so out of concern for Tucker. "I knew it wasn't his fault, and I was determined not to take things out on him," she says. The self-control that Amy developed during this time has helped in other areas of her life as well.

Once the training with Discovery Dogs started, Amy and Tucker attended classes on a regular basis for the next two years. Under Shari's guidance, things improved immediately. Tucker learned basic obedience, as well as tasks specific to Amy's disability. "A blind person's dog isn't a guide dog until it's been taught to guide. An assistance dog must be trained to mitigate its owner's disability," Shari explains.

Tucker's tasks are not as obvious as picking up dropped items or opening doors, but they are equally valuable. For instance, when Amy has been sitting at the computer for too long, she can become obsessive, angry and upset. Tucker breaks the cycle by coming over and putting his head on her lap, forcing her to focus on something outside of herself.

Tucker's very presence has a profound effect on Amy's mood and behavior. "An annoyed exhalation from me can wake the poor guy from a comfortable snooze and make him come over and put his head on my thigh. I feel guilty and don't want to upset him, so I make an effort to stay calm and not get worked up about things."

Amy says Discovery Dogs was wonderful in accommodating her needs. "A lot of other organizations wouldn't have," she is quick to point out. Still, halfway through the training it became clear that Tucker didn't have the personality of a public access dog. He is too headstrong and easily distracted. Amy had two options: She could give up her goal of having Tucker accompany her in public, or she could get another dog. The choice was easy. "There was *no way* I was getting rid of Tucker," Amy declares. "There was just no way."

Amy and Tucker (Photo: Hilary Burns Nishiura)

Although things may not have turned out the way Amy planned, she wouldn't have it any other way. Tucker may not be the perfect dog, but he is perfect for her. "All the reasons that he can't have public access are the things that make him so tremendous: he *is* so active, curious and smart. And he's hilarious. He keeps me on my toes." As for Tucker's stubborn streak – Amy laughs heartily. "It will never get really easy, but we've gotten to the point now where we've negotiated things out."

These days Amy gets plenty of sunshine and exercise. She walks

Tucker at the Presidio, an old army base with scenic views of the Golden Gate Bridge. She continues training Tucker, to keep him calm and mentally sharp. Amy's life has achieved more balance. Her "downs" are not so debilitating and for the first time in years, she has been able to work full time. This is monumental for Amy. The last time she had a full-time job was in 1994, and it only lasted one year.

Tucker isn't the only reason for the dramatic change in Amy's life. She has a network of doctors helping her with medication and therapy, as well as strong family support. But Tucker has had a tremendous influence on her. "He is the best thing that's happened to me. He helps me function as a human being. And one of the best ways he does that is by just *being a dog*." And he keeps her laughing; sometimes so hard that her stomach hurts.

Top Dogs

Mary George was two years old when she was diagnosed with juvenile rheumatoid arthritis. That was only after four doctors and three misdiagnoses. By that time Mary was, according to her parents, a "burning red ball of fire." She had a fever, her joints were swollen and inflamed, and the vertebrae in her neck had fused together so that she was unable to even roll over in bed.

As a child, Mary walked with a limp and took up to 10 aspirin a day just to ease the pain. She longed to be like the other children and often fantasized about sitting on the floor, cross-legged, and playing jacks. But Mary had difficulty even getting down onto the floor, and when she did, she had to sit with her legs straight out and lean on something for support.

Mary felt like an outsider, straddling two different worlds. She was not fully able-bodied, but neither was she disabled enough to use a wheelchair. "I felt like Elvis Presley in the movie "Flaming Star," the one about a young man who was half Indian and half White. I was struggling to fit in. I developed an inferiority complex and felt I had to do more than other people, just to be considered equal to them."

Mary was born and raised in Saginaw, Michigan. After graduating from high school, she moved to Tucson to attend the University of Arizona, and because the warm, dry climate helps to relieve arthritic pain. She adopted Lucky, a small terrier cross, and trained him to help with daily activities. For instance, Lucky learned to pull Mary's pants up to her knee so that she could reach them. He would also retrieve things, then stand on his hind legs and place them in her lap. Much of the training was done by instinct, but Mary also attended local training classes and learned basic principles such as how to use a positive tone of voice. For instance, "When you call Lucky, don't be gruff. Act like he's bringing you a million dollar lottery ticket instead!" she was told.

This experience led Mary, along with four others, to co-found TOP DOG, an organization that teaches disabled individuals how to train their own service dogs. There are several advantages to this approach, she points out. The owner and dog already have a well-developed bond; and the owner develops the confidence and techniques to teach any new skills that may be required should their disability progress.

The late Stewart Nordensson was the inspiration for the organization. Born with cerebral palsy, confined to a power wheelchair and with very restricted speech, his passion was studying, understanding and training dogs. The other founders are Lydia Kelley, Kathy Hurst and Diann Belleranti. Lynn Baker joined the group shortly after it was formed. The group spent close to a year figuring out the nuts-and-bolts of running a non-profit organization, as well as creating application forms and standardizing guidelines and tests.

Around this time, Mary made an important decision concerning Lucky. Although he was well-behaved at home, he tended to snap at people in public, especially if they came up from behind. Because of this, she felt it best to retire him as a service dog, although he would remain a cherished pet, and continue to pick up things and help her dress at home.

Mary started looking for another dog to accompany her in public. Soon afterward, while in the hospital for a hip replacement, she overheard a male nurse talking about his impending divorce. He was moving into a small apartment and had a three-and-a-half-year-old golden retriever named Sage, that he couldn't take with him. The dog desperately needed a new home; if one wasn't found soon, she would be taken to the pound.

While growing up, Mary's family dog had been a "golden." Because of this, the breed held a special place in her heart. Mary arranged to meet the dog, and when she did, she was surprised. Sage had been kept in a backyard all her life. She was timid and terrified of loud noises such as thunder and fireworks. She lacked social skills, and pulled so hard on her leash that she almost knocked Mary over. Still, Mary had a gut feeling that Sage was a very special dog.

Mary and Sage went through the intensive TOP DOG training, which consists of three levels, each taking approximately three months. In the introductory level, the dogs are taught basic obedience; the owners learn about canine behavior such as pack mentality, body language, and how to work with, rather than against, the instincts of their dogs.

In the intermediate level, a dog's obedience skills are fine-tuned. Sage was tested with distractions ranging from strange dogs to people carrying umbrellas, kids running and skipping, and even remote control cars. She also learned tasks like turning on a "touch" lamp, retrieving dropped objects, and standing stiffly at attention so that Mary could use her for support when she was going up and down stairs or curbs.

Mary also took Sage to a mall where she learned to maneuver through a parking lot, obey the *stay* command while being distracted by shopping carts and dropped food, and enter and exit Mary's car in a controlled manner. This last behavior is especially crucial in Mary's case because like many disabled people, she uses a scooter or crutches. Since it is hot in Arizona, she leaves the car door open while loading and unloading her equipment, and it is important that Sage sits quietly on the seat without barking or jumping out of the car.

These skills are necessary in order for dogs to take the Assistance Dogs International's (ADI) Public Access Test. This is a standard exam used by most service organizations to test the dogs' behavior in public. Although Sage didn't take the test, since it was instituted after her training, any dog being certified now is required to pass it.

Top Dog teams then go on to the advanced level, where they practice going out in public to become familiar with a variety of people, situations and sounds. Mary and Sage went to stores, the library, restaurants and the cinema. Teams even go to the Tucson International Airport where they are given boarding passes, go through security, and are "wanded."

Mary and Sage were one of the first teams to be certified by TOP DOG. Since then, many different breeds have gone through the program. There are lots of wonderful shelter crosses and some surprises, too. Golden and Labrador retrievers are strong enough to pull wheelchairs, but some, despite their name, don't like to retrieve. On the other hand a chow chow, which can be quite an aloof breed, unexpectedly turned out to be a fantastic service dog.

Mary and Sage had many wonderful adventures together. While TOP DOG was still a young organization, they attended conferences in St. Louis and Las Vegas. In Montreal they went on the subway; in Hawaii they stayed at an army quarantine station and had animal control officers escort them all over the island. Sage loved to accompany Mary and would get so excited that she would leap in the air like a dolphin. Each time she leapt, Mary would say, "Jump for joy." And eventually Sage started doing it on command.

This trick was a big hit when Mary, along with her friend Cheryl Eneboe, began giving demonstrations at local schools. Cheryl, who was blind, showed the children how her dog Joyce assisted her, and Sage would demonstrate all the service exercises that made Mary's life easier. Afterwards, there was always a lineup of children wanting to pet the dogs. Mary remembers one child, a shy boy of about eight, who stayed to one side tightly holding his teacher's hand. He had been bitten by a dog before and was afraid. But when Sage calmly lay down on the floor, looking more like a welcome mat than a ferocious dog, the boy summoned up his courage and slowly approached. He bent down to pet her, his eyes lit up and he had the biggest smile on his face that Mary had ever seen.

Working with TOP DOG gave Mary increased confidence and self-esteem. She discovered leadership skills that she didn't know she had, and learned to take risks. Not only that, but "Sage gave me unconditional love and made me realize that I was worthy of accepting love from others," Mary says.

One Christmas, Cheryl invited Mary to a party. Mary fully intended to go until she fell and hit her head. "My face was swollen and my eyes were slits," she remembers. "I looked quite frightful, actually." She tried to back out of the party, but Cheryl insisted. And luckily so; because one of the neighbors, Kevin, dropped by.

Mary and Kevin hit it off right away. They soon started dating, and Sage accompanied them to church services and to restaurants.

Mary and Sage (Photo: Lydia Kelley)

Being part of a constant threesome led Kevin to ask, "Does Sage have to go everywhere with us?" "Yes," Mary replied. Then she took Kevin out to dinner and explained the importance of Sage in her life.

By the time the couple got married, Kevin was one of Sage's biggest fans. She was the "flower dog" at the wedding, walking down the aisle carrying a basket of flowers in her mouth. And when Mary arranged for a friend to take Sage while they were on their honeymoon, Kevin was taken aback. "What? She's not coming with us?" he asked. So Sage accompanied them on the day trips they took to Phoenix and the surrounding area.

Mary and Sage were together for 10 years, before the loving dog passed away at the age of 13. "Words aren't adequate to describe what she meant to me," Mary says. "She was truly my once-in-a-lifetime dog."

Mary's current service dog is Liberty, a golden retriever mix. Mary now uses an electric scooter most of the time, and teaches her companion new skills as they become necessary with the progression of her disability.

TOP DOG continues to grow. The organization recently celebrated its 20th anniversary and to date has certified close to 100 service dog teams. Clients range in age from eight to 80 and include those with arthritis, multiple sclerosis, cerebral palsy, muscular dystrophy, spinal cord injuries and numerous other physical disabilities.

Mary says that it is a wonderfully liberating experience to have a service dog, instead of having to rely on others. "Sage expanded my world and brought so much joy into my life." And now, Liberty is doing the same – even though she has some very large paw prints to fill.

Kevin, Mary and their TOP DOGS (Photo: Dennis Brownfield)

PART THREE

Volunteers and Their Dogs

Every Friday night Heather and her rescued collie, Monty, visit seniors at a local care facility. On this particular evening, they were in an Alzheimer's unit when a man bent down, patted Monty, and told Heather she had a beautiful dog. She thanked him, and then she noticed that the staff nurse was crying. The man had not spoken to anyone or acknowledged his surroundings in over a year.

Heather and Monty are just one of over 40,000 pet/handler teams who are members of Therapy Dogs International (TDI®), Therapy Dogs Inc. and Delta Society®, the three main groups that provide testing and set standards for those who volunteer with their pets. Thousands of others are members of smaller national, regional or local organizations. They visit in hospitals, nursing homes, rehabilitation centers and schools, reaching out to millions of people every year.

Delta Society refers to these interactions as "animal-assisted activities" (AAA). This term is used to distinguish the volunteers from those who work in animal-assisted therapy (AAT), which is overseen by a health care professional and works towards a specific clinical goal. Other organizations prefer the term "Therapy Dog." Regardless of the different terminology, a visit from an animal can have significant health benefits, including lower blood pressure and reduced anxiety and stress. There are emotional benefits as well, including increased laughter, greater patient interaction and a marked decrease in depression and loneliness.

For many people who have rescued a dog, volunteering provides an opportunity for them – and their pets – to make a contribution and to give something back. Although the dogs are the star attractions, their handlers are able to witness the transformative power of animals first-hand. They benefit simply by being on the other end of the leash. As one volunteer puts it, "Being constantly greeted with smiles can do wonders for the soul."

Patricia and Lottie Dot (Photo: Marley Richeson)

Lottie Dot

Patricia Belt looks at a photograph of herself, alongside her five-year-old dalmatian Lottie Dot, and can't help but chuckle. Her blue eyes sparkle in the picture and she is obviously very proud. But several wisps of hair have escaped from her upswept hairdo. They flutter at odd angles, some across her face, others straight up into the air. "Oh my, look at that! I'm such a mess!" Patricia exclaims. "I get so caught up with Lottie Dot, I never have time to think about myself, much less stop and comb my hair."

It's no wonder. Lottie Dot is a dog with a multitude of talents, and a chockablock schedule of places to go and people to see. She even has her own resumé, and it is truly an impressive one. Lottie has volunteered in 19 different facilities and received five different awards for her work. As for her interests, they include doing tricks, playing Frisbee, giving hugs and capturing everyone's heart. But what Lottie Dot's resumé doesn't tell you is that when she was only eight weeks old, she was abandoned and almost froze to death in the snow.

Patricia was working as a nurse in California at the time, and her son Stephen was driving out from Missouri for a visit. Patricia wasn't thrilled about the idea. In fact, she was worried. It was the middle of February and winter weather can be extremely unpredictable.

Stephen's trip went smoothly until he reached Oklahoma, and it began to snow. By the time he neared the small town of Catoosa, he found himself in the middle of a ferocious storm. Gale-force winds and slick roads made driving dangerous. The car windows fogged up and it was almost impossible to see.

All of a sudden Stephen saw something lying in the middle of the road. He swerved and brought the car to a screeching stop. He stepped out of the car to investigate and suddenly felt foolish. It was nothing more than a lump of ice and snow. Then the lump moved, ever so slightly. When Stephen hurried over to take a closer look, he could hardly believe his eyes. There, looking up at him, was a tiny puppy. She was frightened, malnourished and trembling from the cold.

Stephen gently picked the puppy up and carried her to the car. He named her Catoosa, after the nearby town where she was found. He bought some milk at a gas station and then drove the rest of the way to California, feeding Catoosa and tucking her under his shirt to keep her warm.

When Stephen arrived in California, he and Patricia took the puppy to the vet. Patricia was worried that Catoosa had wandered off and become lost, and that someone might be looking for her. The vet suspected otherwise. He gave her a BAER (brainstem auditory evoked response) test that measures hearing response and his suspicions were confirmed. Catoosa was completely deaf.

About 12 percent of dalmatians are born deaf, a congenital defect that breeders are determined to eliminate. In fact, the Dalmatian Club of America mandates that all deaf puppies should be euthanized, rather than bred, sold, or given away as pets. The rationale for this, according to club literature, is that deaf dalmatians are difficult to train. They "lack the power of reason and the ability to read a situation and act accordingly," they startle easily and are "potentially dangerous." As a result, they would "lead a sadly neurotic life."

The vet reckoned that a breeder had tested Catoosa and when it was discovered she was deaf, had dumped her on the side of the road. Perhaps the breeder wanted to save the cost of having the pup euthanized, or they didn't want word to get out that they'd bred a "defective" dog.

Patricia and Stephen looked at each other in astonishment. How could anyone label this adorable little puppy as defective? "They were unwilling to have her euthanized, so when the vet suggested using hand signals to train her, they readily agreed. Then they bundled up Catoosa, and took her home to begin her new life.

That night, Patricia marveled at the little pup. "She was so little, and I wanted her close to me always. I would bring her from room to room with me, wherever I went. I wanted her to know she was safe now." Patricia felt that fate had brought Catoosa into her life, and asked Stephen if he might let her keep the dog. Knowing how much it would mean to his mother, Stephen reluctantly agreed. "It's the most wonderful gift he has ever given me," Patricia says.

Patricia started training Catoosa right away. She still remembered the American Sign Language alphabet (ASL) that she had learned while in Girl Scouts. She used the letter "N" for *no* and "S" for *stay*. Other hand signals came naturally, such as holding up a finger to indicate *one minute* when she was going to leave the room.

Catoosa grew more beautiful every day, and her spots kept multiplying. The dainty little pup loved to show off, prancing around the house in what Patricia jokingly calls her "lah-di-dah" way. Then one day at a meet-and-greet outside a grocery store, a young boy with autism approached them. "Lotsa dots," he tried to say, pointing to Catoosa's spotted coat. But his words sounded like "Lottie dot." For Patricia this was a "eureka" moment. Lottie Dot became the puppy's new name.

When Lottie Dot was four months old, Patricia enrolled them both in a Canine Good Citizen (CGC) course, which is run by the American Kennel Club (AKC). The course focuses on responsible pet ownership (like spaying and neutering, and cleaning up after your dog) and good manners for dogs. Because commands were given verbally, after each class Patricia went home and converted them to hand signals. Lottie passed the course two months later, an incredible achievement for such a young dog – and a deaf one at that!

That autumn Patricia was diagnosed with breast cancer (which is now in remission). Her life became a constant round of doctor's appointments and radiation therapy. Since Patricia knew the nurses at the cancer clinic, they let her sneak Lottie Dot in to sit beside her during treatments. This made a huge difference not only to her, but to the other patients as well. Lottie brought joy and laughter into an otherwise bleak world filled with tests, treatments and disease. She gave patients something to focus on, and made time pass more quickly. Lottie seemed to have a sixth sense when it came to reading people's moods. She knew when to be a jester and make everyone laugh, and when to just lie quietly on her blanket and be petted.

The next year Patricia moved to Grand Junction, Tennessee, to be closer to her mother. Grand Junction has a population of 315, and the small-town atmosphere, southern hospitality and close community ties suited Patricia perfectly.

Knowing the impact Lottie had made on her own recovery, Patricia wanted to take her to visit cancer patients at St. Jude Children's Research Hospital in nearby Memphis. She made inquiries and learned that to be able to do this, they would both have to be registered by Delta Society®, an international non-profit society that operates in 50 states and 13 countries worldwide.

Delta Society sets standards for those wishing to participate in animal-assisted activities. It screens, trains and registers volunteers using a "both-ends-of-the-leash" approach, to ensure that both the owners and their pets are well-prepared. Lottie Dot already had her Canine Good Citizen Certification, but in order to volunteer as a Delta Society Pet Partners® team, she and Patricia would have to go back to school.

Patricia attended workshops and enrolled Lottie in a number of training courses. She used the same method as before; going to class with Lottie and then converting the verbal instructions to hand signals at home. Lottie was a quick learner. She soon passed not only the intermediate and advanced training classes, but a "tricks" class as well.

However, when it came time to take the Delta Society evaluation, which was needed in order to be registered, Lottie did not pass and was scored "Not Ready." Twice! There was one particular hurdle that she just couldn't seem to overcome. Patricia had to leave Lottie at one end of a long room, walk across to the other side, then turn around and call her. But Lottie was constantly distracted by the tester instead of watching for Patricia's hand signal. So she just stayed at the other end of the room.

Patricia was undeterred and devised a plan. She practiced walking Lottie on a long leash around the backyard at home. Every time Lottie turned around and made eye contact, Patricia gave her a treat. It wasn't long before she learned to "check in" with Patricia (and get a reward, of course) every 30 seconds or so.

On the day of the third test, Patricia was nervous. She followed the same routine as she had before. She bathed Lottie, brushed her and trimmed her nails. She drove the one-and-a-half hours to the testing center. Then she registered Lottie, led her into the now-familiar room, and held her breath.

Lottie sailed through the first part of the test. She sat, stayed and walked on her leash. She didn't jump up on strangers and was comfortable around wheelchairs and canes. Then came the critical part of the test; Patricia left Lottie on one side of the room, walked to the other side, stopped and turned around. Lo and behold, Lottie was watching! Patricia gave the hand signal for *come* and Lottie responded immediately. She passed the exam! Patricia was understandably proud.

These days Lottie is incredibly busy. She visits St. Jude Children's Research Hospital and various other facilities as well. At a veteran's hospital in Memphis, she assists with physical therapy. Patients with mobility problems walk down the hall with Lottie, who helps them keep their

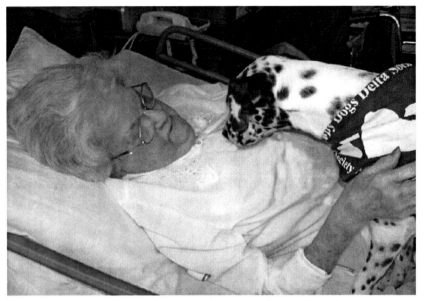

Lottie Dot and patient (Photo: Jennifer Smallwood)

balance. When they take baby steps, she does too; when they take bigger strides, she follows along. She also plays "catch" with patients confined to wheelchairs, which helps them to develop upper body strength. They throw her weighted balls, which she happily retrieves.

Lottie particularly loves children, and the feeling is mutual. On a visit to the Memphis Oral School for the Deaf, she put on a performance for a group of preschoolers. Always the show-off, Lottie balanced a bone on her nose, flipped it and then caught it in her mouth. She jumped through a hula hoop, played peek-a-boo by covering her eyes with her paws and – the children's favorite – after every trick she took a bow!

After the performance, Patricia asked how many of the children thought Lottie could hear. They all put up their hands. When Patricia told them otherwise, stillness settled over the room. They realized that Lottie was just like them, and she could still do amazing things.

Lottie is also part of the Reading Education Assistance Dogs (R.E.A.D.®) program, which aims to improve literacy in children by having them read to a dog. It was started by Sandi Martin and Olivia, her rescued dog. (See "Lessons from Olivia"). In a comprehensive disabilities classroom at Middleton High School, Lottie is one of the favorite teachers. The students, who are between the ages of 14 and 18, always cheer when she enters the classroom. Although some of these students are unable to read complete sentences, Lottie sits beside them encouragingly. She nods with approval when they show her pictures, and even gives them the occasional "high-five." "Lottie can't hear these precious kids read a single word," Patricia says. "She hears in a different way; with her heart. She watches body language and facial expressions and pays close attention to my hand signals."

Reading at Middleton High School (Photo: Jennifer Smallwood)

Nowhere is Lottie's impact more profound than at children's grief camps. These camps are specially designed for those who have lost a parent or close relative in the previous two years. The program combines games and singsongs with activities that help the children explore their feelings and come to terms with their grief.

The dogs aren't part of any scheduled activity at the camps; they are simply available for anyone who wants their support. As Patricia explains, "Children, especially little boys, don't like to talk to counselors. But they sure don't mind talking to a dog."

On the last day of camp, the children compose letters to their loved ones. These letters are attached to memorial balloons and released into the air. One little boy was having trouble putting his thoughts down on paper, but as he petted Lottie, he relaxed and started to write. He even asked Patricia how to spell certain words. "Those words will stay with me until the day I die," Patricia says.

Recently a group of adults who had experienced the loss of a loved one attended the camp. On the first day, an elderly gentleman was sitting alone on a bench with his head in his hands. "When Lottie saw him, she pulled me over to him. She sat next to him and nudged his knee to make him look at her," Patricia recalls. The man had just lost his wife of over 50 years and had been reluctant to attend the camp until his grandchildren, who were in one of the youth groups, convinced him to do so. Lottie and this gentleman spent the next three days together. "With Lottie by his side, he felt more relaxed and comfortable expressing himself during activities and group sessions. He said she was an angel that had been sent to him."

With Lottie's impressive array of accomplishments, it is no wonder that in Grand Junction and the surrounding area she is something of a celebrity. She receives cards and fan letters, sometimes left anonymously in the mailbox, thanking her for the work she does. She's been featured in the local newspaper, and "Lottie Dot" cupcakes (with white icing and chocolate morsels on top) are sold at the bakery. The proceeds go to a special fund to help Patricia, who lives on a small pension, pay for gas so that she and Lottie can continue their animal-assisted activities.

Lottie is also an honorary member of the Grand Junction fire department. She rides on their truck in the Christmas parade, and

Patricia is teaching her to *stop*, *drop* and *roll*, so that she can demonstrate the life-saving technique to schoolchildren. With each new experience, Lottie's repertoire of hand signals expands. She now knows 40 different signals, from *pay attention* to *play dead*. And *thank you*. Patricia uses that one a lot.

Patricia is deeply grateful to have such a special dog in her life, and that she and Lottie are able to spend their days giving back. "We're just doing our little part," she says. "It's why God brought us together."

Patricia often thinks of the miraculous way Lottie came into her life. She will never understand why the Dalmatian Club of America mandates euthanizing deaf dogs. "It's heartbreaking," she says. "Just think of all the Lottie Dots there could be in this world. Think of all the joy that they could bring."

There's a postscript to this story, and a happy one at that. Patricia is getting another puppy; a beautiful, eight-week-old dalmatian named Dora, who is also deaf! A breeder had been accustomed to euthanizing deaf dogs, but in the last litter there was a very special little girl, one that she just couldn't bring herself to put down. She searched for someone to adopt the pup, and after learning about Patricia and Lottie Dot, knew she had found the perfect home. Now Lottie has a new job to add to her resumé – big sister. And if her past accomplishments are any indication, it's safe to assume she'll excel at this, as well.

Mackenzie and Julie (Photo: Gary Turner)

Tornadoes and Hurricanes

I f not for a strange chain of events, Julie Yoder might never have met Mackenzie, a gentle female German shepherd with a loving heart and big brown eyes. Perhaps it was fate; Julie doesn't know for sure, but what is certain is that her life has changed immeasurably. "My world has really opened up," she says. "My own personal mission has expanded and grown. I would like Mackenzie and I to touch as many lives as we can."

Julie, an operations manager with a housewares company, had just moved from an apartment into a house of her own. Located in a suburb of Kansas City it was a real fixer-upper, with a list of things to do that was at least a mile long. But number one on Julie's list wasn't painting or tiling or any other such chore. Instead, she planned on getting the dog she had always wanted, one she could do volunteer work with.

Julie was thinking about getting a German shepherd, when her ex-boyfriend called. He needed to find a new home for Tuesday, his Catahoula leopard dog. True to his breed, Tuesday was energetic and intelligent - traits that Julie felt would make a great therapy dog. And since she already knew and loved Tuesday, she readily agreed to adopt him.

The pair joined the local group of Delta Society® and became a registered Pet Partners® team, but they never got a chance to volunteer. Tuesday died suddenly from what turned out to be an undiagnosed brain disorder.

Devastated, Julie called the organization to explain that she would not be able to volunteer. The woman she spoke with was very sympathetic, allowing Julie to express her feelings and ask a multitude of questions. How could she cope with the sense of loss that she felt? What should she do now? How long should she wait before getting another dog? When Julie mentioned that she'd always wanted a German shepherd, the woman suggested getting in touch with a service organization since some of the dogs that don't make it through the training process are put up for adoption. When Julie hesitated, unbeknownst to her, the woman took control of the situation. After ending the call with Julie, she got in touch with the service organization and told them that Julie was interested in adopting a dog.

Needless to say, Julie was taken by surprise when she received a letter from the service organization, thanking her for her interest and advising her that she had been placed on a waiting list. She was even more surprised when she received a call from Sarah, the president of a local rescue group. Apparently the service organization had forwarded Julie's name to them, along with her "request" to adopt a dog.

Sarah told Julie about a six-month-old pup named Mackenzie that had just been picked up from a high-kill shelter. Like many of the dogs in similar situations, how Mackenzie came to be there can never be verified, but it seems to have been the result of yet another unlikely chain of events.

Apparently a farmer had been looking out his window one morning, when he saw someone driving a truck pull over and dump Mackenzie, along with a young black Lab, onto the road. For weeks, the two dogs ran loose, foraging for any scraps they could find. The farmer began to put food out to keep them alive, and when someone eventually adopted the Lab, he decided to take Mackenzie to the shelter, hoping that someone there would be able to help. The workers at the shelter realized what a nice dog she was and called Sarah, who had previously fostered several of their dogs and helped to find them good homes. Sarah agreed to foster Mackenzie until a suitable placement could be found. A few days later she learned that Julie was looking for a dog.

When Sarah contacted her, Julie was torn. Tuesday had just died, and she felt the timing just wasn't right. She wondered if she was ready to let another dog into her heart so soon. But on the other hand, here was a wonderful animal desperately in need of a home. Then Sarah said something that resonated deeply with Julie: "It is possible to grieve and love at the same time."

Julie decided to meet Mackenzie, and when she did, she was overwhelmed. "I saw her face, and there was something in her eyes that I fell in love with," Julie recalls. "You know how people love their dogs and say they are beautiful, no matter what? Well, Mackenzie was, and is, the most beautiful dog I have ever seen."

There was one catch. Julie had previously planned a vacation to Florida with some friends from work. So Sarah agreed to continue fostering Mackenzie until Julie returned home. In the meantime, the two women corresponded regularly and became very close. As Julie says, "I ended up gaining not one, but two best friends."

When Julie returned from vacation, Mackenzie moved into her new home. As it turns out, that was the last "real" vacation Julie has had. She and Mackenzie now spend all their weekends and vacation time on call-outs at tornado, hurricane and other disaster sites. "It's not as relaxing, but it's far more rewarding," she says.

Julie and Mackenzie are volunteers with National Animal Assisted Crisis Response (AACR), a nonprofit organization that trains dogs and their handlers to deal with the unique challenges of disaster response. The training involves stress management, grief counseling, and how to be effective and professional in stressful and highly unpredictable environments. Once certified, team members provide comfort and support to both disaster victims and first responders, such as police officers, firefighters and paramedics.

"Animal-assisted crisis response is relatively new and a lot of people don't understand what it is that we do," Julie tells me. "It's not show-and-tell with your dog. It's not 'here's my cute dog, do you want to pet her?' The mental health component is an important part of healing. We've heard a number of times that what we do can be very helpful for those going through difficult experiences. If we can take away a little bit of that trauma, if we can help make the process a little easier, that's a meaningful thing in people's lives."

This was evident on the trip that Julie and Mackenzie, along with two other AACR teams, took to Louisiana six weeks after Hurricane Katrina ripped through the state, leaving devastation in its wake. The group had been invited by the Board of Education in Franklinton, a rural, economically depressed region about 60 miles north of New Orleans. Like most of their trips, this one was self-funded. They traveled 15 hours in a donated van and stayed in the battered, but still livable house of a friend.

The area had been pounded by 167-mph winds, with gusts of 190 mph and up to nine feet of water and sludge. Many homes had been completely destroyed, and a large percentage of those left standing were covered with tarps. Julie recalls driving down a two-lane highway and seeing a shack with a big uprooted tree sticking out of a window, and children playing on the lawn. "People were living in houses that normally would be inhabitable," Julie says. "But they had no choice."

The residents were feeling frustrated, angry and abandoned. Resources were being channeled to more populated areas first. As a result, there was still no power, and many of the roads were blocked with mud and debris. For an entire week Mackenzie, Julie and their teammates visited nursing homes and schools, providing "emotional first aid." They let residents know they hadn't been forgotten, and that somebody cared.

The response from the residents was overwhelming. Their first day in Louisiana, Julie and Mackenzie visited an elementary school and saw a little girl around ten years old, wandering the halls in tears. She had been evacuated from another area; this was her first day at a new school. Class had already started, the doors were closed, there were no windows and she was afraid to go inside.

Julie and Mackenzie walked with her to the end of the hallway and the three of them sat in an alcove. The little girl hugged Mackenzie and began to calm down. Julie told her she knew it was scary, and that she was being very brave. Then Julie and Mackenzie walked her back down the hall and into her classroom where she became an

Mackenzie in New Orleans (Photo: Julie Yoder)

instant "rock star" because of the dog. "We couldn't bring back her house or replace what she had lost, but we made her feel a bit better. And that's something," Julie says.

That week the teams visited several other schools, distributing teddy bears, as well as trading cards (similar to those of baseball players) with pictures and "fun facts" about the dogs. Mackenzie's trading card has a regal-looking picture of her on one side; the other side reveals that her favorite color is purple, her tricks are crossing her paws and taking a nap, her favorite treats are liver brownies and peaches, and she likes squeaky toys, the water hose, and popping bubble wrap!

The children were not used to having "special visitors" and raced over for a chance to pet and hug their new furry friends. "It was very emotional," Julie recalls, "particularly for the parents and teachers who were struggling just to keep it together. Some of them cried when they saw how well the children were interacting with the dogs."

The visits to the nursing homes were equally appreciated. The residents were doing fine physically, but were emotionally distraught. Many didn't know the condition of their homes or the whereabouts of family and friends. A visit from Mackenzie and her teammates was a welcome surprise. "I can't believe you came all this way just to see us," was a common response.

"Mackenzie has an innate need to connect with people," Julie says. "In human terms, she's the type of girl who wants to pull up a chair and have a long chat." Although crisis response work can be physically and emotionally draining, "Mackenzie is rock solid. Sometimes she leads me to someone I otherwise would not have approached and it turns out that's the person who needs us the most. I believe that at times our dogs tune into human emotions better than we do."

About a year after becoming certified AACR team members, Julie and Mackenzie joined NOAH's Canine Crisis Response Team, a regional crisis response group based in Crete, Nebraska, which responds to emergency situations in Kansas, Missouri, Iowa and other neighboring states. "There aren't really any physical boundaries to where we go," Julie says. "The only boundaries we have are determined by how many vacation days we have left and how far we can drive." One of these trips took them to the Westroads Mall in Omaha, Nebraska, on a cold and blustery day in December, 2007.

Three days earlier, as the mall buzzed with Christmas shoppers and cheerful carols filled the air, a 19-year-old man wearing an over-sized sweatshirt entered the Von Maur department store. He took the elevator to the third floor, pulled out a concealed AK-47 semi-automatic weapon and fired 30 shots into the crowd, before turning the gun on himself. Nine people were killed, four were wounded, and an entire town was traumatized by this violent, senseless act.

When the mall reopened the following Saturday, it was evident that a concerted effort had been made to help customers and staff feel safe and secure. Members of the police force were in attendance everywhere and security guards manned the entrances. The Red Cross and The Salvation Army offered complimentary coffee and donuts, and grief counselors were also available.

Julie and Mackenzie were there, along with three other crisis response teams, to escort employees as they headed back to work. Emotions were incredibly high and people clasped onto the dogs for support. One woman dissolved in tears as she approached the mall. Another stood at the door for fifteen minutes before finding the strength to go inside.

A lot of people went to the mall that day. Some were there to shop, but the majority had come simply to show their support. They brought paper snowflakes with the names of the victims written on them to hang on the Christmas tree in the food court. Von Maur remained closed and its windows were blacked out, but a memorial was set up outside the store with teddy bears, flowers, candles and more paper snowflakes. "The whole town banded together," Julie says. "They decided the shooting wasn't going to define them or destroy their holiday spirit. But most didn't realize how incredibly difficult the experience would be."

Throughout the day, Julie and Mackenzie, along with their teammates, mingled with the customers and staff, listening to their stories and offering comfort and support. One woman had worked at Von Maur for ten years and the shooting had occurred on her day off. Her grief was combined with survivor's guilt because several of her co-workers had been injured or killed. A young couple had heard the gunshots ring out across the mall and ran into a storage room, locking the door. They had no idea how much time had passed before they heard someone pounding on the door. They couldn't hear any voices and were terrified. Was it the police or the gunman on the other side of the door?

While outside on a much needed break, Mackenzie started scratching in the snow on the sidewalk. "She's not a digger, but she kept pawing at something," Julie says. She looked closer and saw a splash of blood on the ground. "That was when I realized just how horrific it must have been."

One of the most moving experiences occurred during a rare, quiet moment when Julie saw a young man standing by himself at the memorial in front of the Von Maur store. "We rarely intrude on someone's private grief," Julie tells me, "but something made me speak to this man." She went over and asked if he would like to hug Mackenzie. The man bent down, buried his face in Mackenzie's fur and began to cry. Then he looked up at Julie and simply said, "Thanks, I needed that," before walking away.

Julie is quick to praise her teammates, peppering conversations with their stories, as well as her own. And she is continually impressed by the work other organizations do. "We're not mental health workers, but we have disaster mental health training and are taught to look for signs of post-traumatic stress disorder (PTSD). In disaster situations, there are always times when we need the assistance of the Red Cross and The Salvation Army personnel, and they are always there."

That Saturday night, Julie, Mackenzie and their teammates drove back home in the middle of an ice storm. They had only been in Omaha for one day, but it had been their most intense experience so far. "People let us into their nightmare," Julie says. "I feel honored to have shared their grief."

Animal-assisted crisis response teams provide emotional support not only for victims of disasters, but for first responders as well. This was the case in Parkersburg, Iowa, a small rural community of about 1,000 that had been demolished by an F5 tornado in May 2008. Seven people were killed and 50 injured in the wake of the disaster, and nearly 200 homes were damaged or destroyed. Julie and Mackenzie visited the area, alongside several other NOAH's crisis response teams. They went out into the "debris field" to comfort survivors who were sifting through their possessions and what was left of their homes. But much of their time was spent at the fire station, providing a little canine comfort to the first responders who congregated there.

Julie and Mackenzie have taken a Critical Incident Stress Management (CISM) course to prepare them for dealing with situations like this. "The critical incident was the tornado; stress management is how they deal with the aftermath," Julie explains. "We go through a set list of procedures that help first responders deal with what they've been through."

Mackenzie with First Responders
(Photo: Julie Yoder)

A visit from a dog can boost morale, reduce feelings of stress and isolation, and provide a sense of normalcy for those missing their families and pets back home. "These guys have to go out and see unimaginable things every day," Julie explains. "They can't let their guard down; people are counting on them. Physically connecting with another creature who is giving them complete and unconditional love eases their burden a little. It helps them go out and do it all over again the next day."

Julie remains modest about the work they do. "We're not heroes," she is quick to point out. "We're not saving babies from burning buildings and we're not rebuilding towns. But I hope we make the job a little bit easier for those who do."

Of course, Julie and Mackenzie need a way to decompress too. "Like humans, dogs can take on emotions, heartache and pain, which can be draining," Julie says. "In our training, we learn how to take care of ourselves and take care of our dogs." She keeps a journal and talks about her thoughts, feelings and experiences with other members of her team. Mackenzie's process is entirely different. She runs around and has a good romp, then crashes and sleeps like a log!

Julie is incredibly passionate and dedicated to crisis response. The work has given her a sense of purpose and taught her about the healing power of dogs. These days, she spends all her vacation time either at disaster sites or in classes and training sessions with her favorite canine by her side. Her holiday to Florida, which she took before adopting Mackenzie, seems like a long ago dream.

I admire Julie's commitment, although I can't help but wonder: Wouldn't she like to take another "real" vacation? Perhaps to another beach somewhere? Julie laughs at this question. "Yeah, I'd love to. A beach sounds really nice." Then she adds, without missing a beat, "But you know, this work is what Mackenzie and I are called to do."

Dr. Leo

On April 25, 2007, Marthina McClay was relaxing in her living room watching television, when a news flash was broadcast. Property owned by National Football League (NFL) star Michael Vick had been raided, and approximately 50 pit bulls that were allegedly part of a dog fighting operation had been seized. Marthina sat bolt upright, stunned. "I don't believe it," was the first thought that went through her mind.

The news clip went on to show an animal control officer standing in front of a kennel beside a tan-colored, muscular pit bull. When the dog turned its head Marthina caught a glimpse of its "beautiful, kohl-rimmed, Maybelline eyes" and she couldn't help but think, "Oh my God! What a beautiful dog!"

Marthina is the founder and president of Our Pack, Inc., a Los Gatos, California-based group that rescues and advocates for pit bulls. A certified dog trainer and animal behavioral consultant, she is also involved in animal-assisted activities, and has visited nursing homes with Hailey, her five-year-old brindle pit bull, for the past several years.

"I would really love to get one of those dogs and train it to do therapy work," she thought to herself. "That would be the best testament to the breed that America will ever see." But she knew that dogs seized in "fight bust" cases are almost always euthanized once they are no longer needed as "evidence" in court. It is assumed that they are menacing, dangerous and out of control. "It's such a shame," Marthina concluded. "People will never know what these dogs are capable of." Fortunately, she was wrong.

Michael Vick lived a rags-to-riches story. Born and raised in a poor, crime-ridden neighborhood in Newport News, Virginia, he attended college on a football scholarship. He then went on to a professional NFL career as the record-breaking quarterback for the Atlanta Falcons. At the age of 24, he signed one of the biggest contracts in NFL history. That, combined with lucrative commercial endorsements, landed him in the number 19 spot on the 2005 Forbes' list of highest paid celebrities.

To all outward appearances, Michael Vick seemed to be living the American Dream. But away from the media spotlight, he was part of a multi-million dollar subculture. Vick owned the Bad Newz Kennels, which was located on his 15-acre rural property in Smithville, Virginia. For six years he, along with two friends, ran an illegal dog fighting operation there.

When police and animal control workers raided Vick's property, they found dogs housed in little more than hovels or tied to car axles with heavy, logging-type chains. They also found blood-stained carpets and evidence of animal remains. Investigators later learned that the dogfights went on for hours, and dogs that did not perform well were brutally executed by electrocution, hanging, drowning, or by being repeatedly slammed to the ground.

Public outrage was swift and deep. Vick was suspended from the NFL following the flood of angry protest letters to the league, and sponsorship endorsements quickly evaporated or were withdrawn. "Breeding and training dogs to fight to the death is the ultimate betrayal of our oldest relationship with animals," Stephen Zawistowski says. Steven is the executive vice president of the American Society for the Prevention of Cruelty to Animals (ASPCA)®. "The Michael

Vick case helped to shine a brilliant light on an activity that has long lurked in the shadows. It forced people to take notice that a cruel practice thought to have been relegated to the past is still with us."

On August 24, 2007, Michael Vick entered into a plea agreement in which he admitted to taking part in a dogfight operation and to actively participating in killing dogs that did not perform well. In December, Vick was sentenced to 23 months in jail. And, for the first time in history, federal agents, the district attorney's office, several animal shelters and animal law experts worked together in what would become a landmark animal welfare case.

Judge Henry E. Hudson ordered that each pit bull be evaluated individually, rather than being automatically destroyed. In an ironic twist, the cost of taking care of the dogs was to be covered by Vick. As part of the plea agreement, Vick was required to pay $928,073.04 restitution to the dogs for expenses incurred, including long-term care and/or humane euthanasia, if deemed necessary. The use of the term "restitution" was significant, as it acknowledged that the dogs were victims of animal abuse, rather than lethal fighting machines.

At the beginning of September, Zawistowski assembled a nine-person team consisting of ASPCA staff, outside behavioral specialists and members of the rescue group BAD RAP (Bay Area Doglovers Responsible About Pit bulls) to conduct evaluations on the confiscated dogs. Team members had absolutely no idea what to expect when they began their task. The dogs had not only been subjected to horrendous conditions at the Bad Newz Kennels, their next four months had been spent in isolation at animal control facilities, because they were believed to be dangerous.

The pit bulls were first tested to see if they would tolerate human handling. Team members found surprisingly little aggression. Many of the dogs were fearful or shy; some had obviously been abused, and cowered in their kennels with their heads down, their tails between their legs. The pit bulls were then tested for aggression towards other dogs. Some showed signs of aggression, but their attention could be refocused. Others were cautious. But many were well-mannered and friendly, even wagging their tails and wanting to play.

The importance of judging each dog as an individual, rather than on the basis of stereotypical "breed profiling" soon became clear. Only one pit bull was so aggressive towards humans and other animals that she was considered dangerous and had to be euthanized. (One other dog was euthanized because she was ill and in pain and there was nothing that could be done medically to help her.)

A few months after Vick's arrest, Marthina read a follow-up newspaper article stating that the confiscated pit bulls were being saved. Rebecca Huss, a nationally recognized expert in animal law at the Valparaiso University School of Law in Indiana, was named guardian/special master to the dogs. Rebecca determined that the dogs should be placed with rescue organizations, which would provide rehabilitation and training, with the possibility of future adoption.

Marthina was astonished. She immediately contacted Rebecca, submitted an application, and went through an extensive screening process. Applicants needed to have insurance and prove they had a certain level of experience working with pit bulls, among other standards. After Marthina was approved, she asked Rebecca if any of the dogs had the potential to do therapy work. There were several candidates; Rebecca sent her a video of Leo, a handsome, tan-colored, two-year-old with deep brown eyes. "To this day, I swear it was the same dog I saw on TV," Marthina says. "Leo looked so eager and friendly. I could imagine cartoon 'thought bubbles,' with him saying 'I'm the guy for you! Take me now.'"

Leo had not been socialized when he first came to live with Marthina. "I don't think he'd ever seen a couch before. He didn't understand what toys were, or a warm bed, or a bone," she recalls. "It's not that he wasn't friendly; he just didn't understand about love, or what he was here for." Leo was "kennel crazy" from having been cooped up

Marthina and Leo (Photo: Stephanie Lam)

most his life. "He acted like a caveman at a tea party. He was like a four-month-old puppy, jumping up on people and nipping their clothes. He had no manners or social skills and was literally bouncing off walls."

Leo paced a lot to relieve anxiety. He traveled from the kitchen to the living room to the dining room, then back again. Marthina used calming techniques such as speaking to him in a low voice, putting on soft music and dimming the lights. She would sit beside Leo, petting him and trying to get him to relax. She kept a diary during this time and about ten days after she brought him home, she wrote: "Wow! A big win! He sat down beside me for the count of five."

Marthina used positive reinforcement such as hugs, kisses and lots of praise; things that Leo had never experienced before. He loved training, and quickly learned obedience skills and how to walk on a leash. "You could see the love, affection and intelligence while Leo was training. When he figured out how to do something, he'd have this expression on his face that seemed to be saying 'Hey! I get it!' as if he were very proud."

All this hard work paid off. Leo aced his Canine Good Citizen test and was then tested and certified by Therapy Dogs, Inc. He accomplished all of this in just five weeks, which is an extremely short period of time. "It's a testament to the breed," Marthina tells me. Pit bulls are resilient. "They bounce back. They don't hold grudges. They're not sitting on The Jerry Springer Show, mopping their brow and saying, 'Oh, I can't move forward with my life.'"

These days "Dr. Leo," as he is affectionately called, visits a number of different facilities. In a calm and gentle manner, he carefully approaches patients while expertly maneuvering around breathing tubes and IVs. Leo never jumps up on patients or puts up his paw. Instead, he waits patiently to be petted, or for a lap on which to plunk down his big, friendly head.

Leo often wears a clown collar when he visits because, as Marthina puts it, "Pit bulls are clowns, they really are. They provide therapy for people who are ill or depressed. They want to be with somebody, even if they're scary looking." Although some people are initially afraid of pit bulls, even if they have never met one, Leo quickly wins them over. "He is magnetic, a real Casanova. Leo is a darling, darling dog."

One of the first places Marthina and Leo visited was a convalescent home for Alzheimer's patients. When they arrived, patients were sitting around the fireplace in a big reception area. There was a lot of activity going on, yet Marthina noticed one woman sitting in the middle of the room, staring blankly at the wall. Leo was in the woman's peripheral vision and she slowly turned her head, looked at him and gave a little crook of a smile. On the way out, a receptionist stopped Marthina to tell her this woman never responded to anything. This was the first time in years there had been a sparkle in her eyes.

Leo also visits patients undergoing chemotherapy at the Camino

Medical Group (CMG) in Mountain View, California. The staff takes a "doggie break" instead of a coffee break when they see him coming down the hall. And the patients are always happy when "Dr. Leo" makes his rounds.

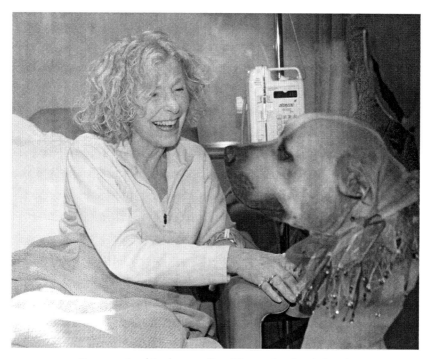

Leo wearing his clown collar (Photo: Stephanie Lam)

Marthina waits until patients get to know Leo before telling them about his past. "Him? A fight dog?" is the usual, stunned response. It's hard for them to reconcile a "tough dog" image with the goofy dog sitting in front of them, wagging his tail and batting his big brown eyes. When they look closer at the scars behind Leo's ears, they find the telltale signs of the abuse he endured.

This is often a pivotal moment for patients. One woman said she would never again feel sorry for herself after learning what Leo had been through. Other times, people reach out and hug the gentle dog. "There is a common bond between Leo and the patients," Marthina says. "They are both survivors. They have both faced off against death. Leo lets them know that anything is possible. He gives them the strength to go on."

Marthina says pit bulls are especially suited to this type of work. "It's really in their temperament to be soft and cuddly and affectionate with people. That's how they are at their core."

"Soft" is one word many pit bull owners use to describe their dogs, in addition to "goofball," "dork" and "clown." That's a far cry from the fear, the breed bans, and the media headlines that scream "PIT BULL ATTACKS!"

Pit bulls haven't always been given the label of "most dangerous dog." (That dubious distinction belonged to bloodhounds in the 19th century, then German shepherds, dobermans and rottweilers after that.) For decades, pit bulls were actually regarded as "America's sweethearts." In the Civil War era, they were referred to as "nanny dogs" because they were so good with children. During World War I, they became symbols of courage, loyalty and resilience; they were used on advertising billboards to sell everything from war bonds, to RCA Records and Buster Brown shoes. In the 1950s Little Petey, a white pit bull with a black circle around one eye, became the star of "The Little Rascals," a children's comedy show. So what happened?

Some cite July 27, 1987, as a major turning point in the downward spiral of the breed's reputation. That month, the headline on the cover of *Sports Illustrated* read: "Beware of this dog." Underneath was a photograph of a snarling, open-mouthed, ferocious-looking pit bull. As Jim Gorant wrote in a later issue of the magazine (December 28, 2008), "The cover cemented the dogs' badass cred, and as rappers affected the gangster ethos, pit bulls became cool. Suddenly, any thug or wannabe thug knew what kind of dog to own."

Pit bulls became front-page news, characterized as vicious, uncontrollable, unpredictable animals. Myths sprang up: pit bulls have locking jaws (they do not – it would be physically impossible); their brains swell and never stop growing (ditto). And perhaps most damaging of all: that pit bulls are immune to pain.

These erroneous beliefs, often encouraged by media hysteria, contradict evidence that supports Marthina's assessment of the breed. The American Temperament Test Society, Inc. (ATTS), which uses standardized test criteria to measure temperament across different breeds, found that Labs have the best scores, with 92 percent passing. But what might be surprising to some is that pit bulls rate at a respectable 85.3 percent, higher than golden retrievers, cocker spaniels, poodles, collies and many other family favorites. As for dog attacks, the majority of incidents reported by the media are the result of irresponsible pet ownership (the dogs are not properly cared for, they are abused, neglected, or trained as guard dogs).

Marthina believes that education will help change negative stereotypes about this breed. For that reason, she was thrilled when school officials invited her to visit a juvenile facility that provides temporary housing for youths in trouble with the law. Several of the students there had been boasting about dog fighting, and the officials were concerned.

When Marthina entered the room, some of the students took one look at Leo and made comments like, "Man, that's a badass dog." Marthina didn't respond. Instead, she proceeded to walk around the room, introducing Leo and inviting the students to pet him.

As Leo worked his magic, Marthina and the teacher took an informal survey. They discovered that all of the students were aware of dog fighting, and that almost half had either attended a dogfight or knew someone who had. When the teacher revealed that Leo was a "Michael Vick dog" there was a stunned silence. They had just been petting and playing with him; how could that possibly be?

"You can't just stand there and preach to kids about how to treat dogs in a humane way," Marthina says. "When you get them in front of a dog like Leo, and he is leaning on them, licking them, and wanting to be petted and hugged, they can see the affinity he has for people, which makes a huge difference. They couldn't imagine that someone ever treated Leo that way."

During the discussion that followed, Marthina told the students that people who fight dogs are cowards. "If you have a problem with someone and want to fight, that's your choice. Go outside and duke it out for yourself, but don't make your dog fight your battles for you. That's a cowardly thing to do." The probation officer later wrote to Marthina, thanking her for making this point.

Marthina later returned to the school to show the students how to train pit bulls using positive reinforcement. She hopes these interactions will help them regard animals as the feeling, sentient beings they are.

Leo and students (Photo: Stephanie Lam)

Marthina is aware that people who hear Leo's story may think he is an exception to the rule. "But Leo is not a one-off," she says. Many dogs with horrendous backgrounds go on to become amazing healers. Zoe, another pit bull rescued by Our Pack, Inc., is a case in point.

Zoe's owner, Cindy Duncan, fell in love with the dog from the first moment they met. "She crawled into my lap, and into my heart, the first night I brought her home," she says. Zoe visits convalescent homes. "She just shines. Whenever she sees a dog or a person, her ears go back and her butt starts wiggling and she moves forward to meet them. It's the funniest sight – she just dances with joy. That's what makes her a great therapy dog. She's just thrilled to meet everybody; she is incredibly sweet."

Zoe was rescued in another dog fighting investigation, which occurred in the wake of the Micheal Vick case. Because of all the press surrounding that case, the public has become more aware of the barbaric practice of dog fighting, which has resulted in more tips to the police and, subsequently, more raids. There is also a growing recognition of the need to evaluate each dog as an individual, rather than automatically labeling them as vicious and sentencing them to death.

It is an uphill battle. Pit bull bans remain in effect in many cities and towns. But perhaps things are changing for this misunderstood breed. The December, 2008 cover of *Sports Illustrated* featured a pit bull once again, only this time the headline read "The Good News Out of the Bad Newz Kennels" and the photo showed "Sweet Jasmine," a chocolate-colored pit bull with a wistful expression and deep, soulful eyes. Jasmine was one of the dogs rescued from Vick's property who has now found a new life and a happy home.

As for Leo, Marthina often wonders if Michael Vick will ever see a picture of him wearing his clown collar. And if he does, will he even realize what a special dog he is? "Leo is a lover, not a fighter," she says.

It takes a moment for this to sink in. Leo is not aggressive; he doesn't have the "chops" for fighting. If not for that police raid, he likely would have died a cruel and painful death.

Leo doesn't worry about these things. He is too busy enjoying his new life. His days are filled with lots of love, toys and plenty of time for play. "He's a clown. He's probably the most clownish of all my dogs. It's amazing, when you consider where he came from," Marthina says. "He likes to clown around. He'll jump halfway on the couch, miss it and then fall backwards with his legs sticking straight in the air." He thoroughly enjoys his work as a "therapy" dog. And at the end of the day, he loves nothing more than to put up his feet, conk out on the couch and snore!

Letters Between Friends

Those who knew Sean Flanagan describe him as a wonderful, conscientious, caring young man. He was a good student who loved photography, watching the Discovery Channel and girls. He was also an avid sportsman, passionate about kayaking. It was on the river negotiating the rapids that he felt most alive.

Sean's mother, Laura, is a dental assistant; his father, David, is a firefighter. His sister, Kelsey, was born when Sean was four years old. The Flanagans are an exceptionally close-knit family. "We always did things together," Laura recalls. "We enjoyed being around each other so much." In fact, when Laura and David were scheduled to visit friends in Australia for three weeks to celebrate their 20th wedding anniversary, they made a last-minute decision. Realizing that they didn't want to be away from their children for that long, they brought them along. "We're so thankful that we had that time to share as a family," Laura tells me, "and for the great memories we have."

The trip was in July. Three months later, at the age of 17, Sean was diagnosed with Ewing sarcoma, a rare and aggressive form of cancer that occurs in the soft tissues and bones. The disease most frequently affects young males between 10 and 20 years of age.

Much of the family's next year was spent at the Children's Hospital in Denver. Sean lost his right leg due to a malignant tumor, and underwent biweekly chemotherapy sessions and bone marrow transplants. His parents were constantly by his side. They would trade off, spending alternate nights at the hospital, and going to work directly from there the following morning.

The family relied on their strong faith in God, and on each other. Sean remained positive. "He had a wry sense of humor and an impish smile," Laura recalls. "He was always trying to encourage us and make us laugh."

Still, Sean was lonely. The oncology unit is a very sterile place. Animals cannot visit and even live plants are not allowed. Sean missed his dog, Sandy, an energetic beagle. And aside from spending time with his family, he had little contact with the outside world. So when Anne Ingalls Gillespie, a pediatric oncology nurse at the Children's Hospital in Denver, told Sean about Youth and Pet Survivors (YAPS), he was intrigued.

YAPS pairs children and teens who are undergoing chemotherapy with animals who have survived cancer. They become "pen pals," communicating by letter or e-mail. The program was founded by Anne, along with Colleen Chambers, a surgical technician at the Veterinary Referral Center of Colorado (VRCC). They believe that young cancer patients can develop supportive and meaningful relationships with animals that have undergone similar experiences. Children can often share thoughts, feelings and fears with an animal in a way they are unable to with their parents, doctors or friends.

Sean looked through a portfolio that contained photos and biographies of the participating dogs. When he came across a picture of Boone, he immediately knew he wanted this happy-go-lucky yellow Lab as his pen pal. Like Sean, Boone loves the outdoors. His favorite pastime is wandering the 75 acres of woodlands and pastures surrounding the place he and Connie Fredman, his constant companion and friend, call home. But Boone and Sean have something else in common as well. They are both amputees.

Connie and Boone live in Fort Collins, Colorado, a city 50 miles north of Denver nestled in the foothills of the Rocky Mountains. Fort Collins is home to the Colorado State University (CSU), as well as the College of Veterinary Medicine and Biomedical Sciences (CVMBS), one of the leading veterinary teaching hospitals in the world. Its renowned oncology department provides chemotherapy and radiation treatments to animals from all across the United States.

Connie runs the Canine Health Resort, a home away from home for animals who have traveled from other areas to undergo medical treatment here. The "guests" have free range of her house and property, and at night they each have a cozy bed of their own. There is plenty of fresh air, along with good food, exercise and an abundance of love. Connie provides solace for animals that would otherwise be lonely, traumatized and afraid; and peace of mind for their owners, who know their pets are being well cared for. The resort has its own special welcoming committee consisting of an assortment of horses, dogs and cats. And, of course, there is Boone, who acts as chief "tail-wagger" and canine mentor. (When he's not rolled over on his back in his trademark belly-rub position, that is!) But Boone's place of honor at the resort was not always assured. It was only through the kindness of strangers that he came to be here.

Boone was born in a neighboring state. Connie won't say exactly where, and she has a good reason, which will soon become clear. Boone's previous owners let him run loose, even though there were busy roads nearby. When he was three years old the inevitable happened: he was hit by a car. Boone's brachial plexus nerve, which runs down his spine and into his limbs, was badly damaged. As a result, his left front leg dragged on the ground. Boone was clearly in pain, but his owners didn't take him to the vet until six to eight weeks later, when horrible sores had developed on his foot.

By that time Boone's leg was so badly damaged that the vet said it would have to be amputated. The owners asked how much the operation would cost, and when they were told it would cost six hundred dollars, they balked. "Forget it," they said. "For that amount of money, we could buy ourselves another dog." They instructed the vet to euthanize Boone, signed the necessary papers and left the office without looking back.

The vet was stunned. He could not possibly bring himself to put such a magnificent animal down. The vet discussed the matter with his staff, and together they decided to help the dog. They would raise money to pay for the surgery, which would be performed "at cost," and to provide for his pre- and post-operative care. Then, when Boone was well enough to travel, they would relocate him to another state. This was deemed a necessary precaution; the owners had signed papers authorizing euthanasia, not surrender papers, so the vet did not have legal guardianship.

One of the technicians at the clinic, who had previously worked in Colorado, knew Connie and gave her a call. Connie was deeply moved by Boone's plight and agreed to foster him after the surgery, and then help find him a good home. She also set about raising money for Boone's care by putting flyers all across town – at the Holiday Inn, a doggie daycare and even a local microbrewery. "Fort Collins is an incredibly dog-friendly town," Connie enthuses. "It was incredible. People donated what they could - from one dollar to $50. In one week we had collected over $600 without anyone even seeing a picture of Boone!"

Boone's operation and recovery went well. Six days after the surgery, on a snowy Thursday afternoon, Connie and the technician each drove halfway along the interstate highway and met at a rest stop. Then, in a scene reminiscent of an old spy movie, Boone was bundled from one car to the other. Then Connie drove back to Colorado, successfully transferring the "refugee" across the state line.

Two days after bringing Boone home, Connie realized that he wasn't going to be staying *just* until he recovered. She was going to adopt this dog! Connie already had an eight-year-old yellow Lab named Ozzie, and her roommate had Quincy, another yellow Lab. "Boone fit in perfectly with these two other dogs," Connie says. "It was like he had lived here all his life. I looked at him and realized he was now part of the family."

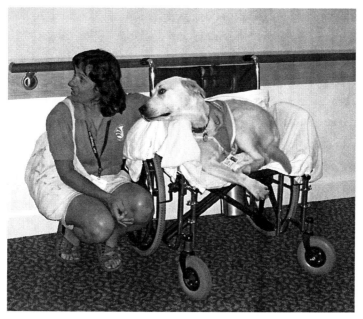

Connie and Boone (Photo: Lyn Perdue)

Boone's sutures took about two weeks to heal. Learning to navigate on three legs, rather than four, took much longer. Connie walked with Boone in the pastures surrounding her house, allowing him to go at his own pace, and his strength and endurance quickly improved. As Connie watched him heal, she came to a decision. So many people had reached out to help Boone; she wanted to find a way to give back.

Boone and Connie were soon registered as a Pet Partners® team with Delta Society® and now visit schools and hospitals throughout the area. With his wagging tail and cheerful demeanor, Boone inspires and motivates everyone he meets. He also became a blood donor at the CSU Veterinary Teaching Hospital. After everything Boone's been through, he doesn't mind the occasional needle prick, knowing that a treat is sure to follow.

While Connie was visiting a friend in the hospital, she saw a photograph of a young cancer patient petting a dog. After making some inquiries she discovered they were members of YAPS. Boone had never had cancer, but because he was an amputee, Connie felt he had something important to offer. She contacted Anne, who readily agreed.

Like all pet owners who wish to participate, Connie was interviewed and carefully screened. Owners need to be responsible, creative and fun, as well as emotionally able to handle a relationship with a sick child. They also need to be willing to provide their pets with a little "secretarial help."

Soon after that, Sean chose Boone as his pen pal. Sean's first e-mail to Boone is touchingly sincere:

Dear Boone,

> *I am doing really well now and plan on going to get my prosthetic fit real soon. There's not much else about my med life.*

> *I really enjoy kayaking as well as snowboarding. I have a really good friend named Brad; he is a pro kayaker and runs a cancer camp for kids. The camp teaches kids that once you put your mind to something, you can do just about anything you want. All the kids learn how to kayak at camp as well as team-building skills. It will be a blast when I go, except Brad will put me to work, seeing I already know how to kayak, but no big deal. As long as I'm doing what I love.*

After all this is over, I plan to become a wildland fire-fighter, if possible. But if not, there is always something I can do to make me happy.

Until next time,
Sean Flanagan

Sean knew, of course, that he wasn't actually communicating with a dog. Still, it gave him a sense of security and allowed him to open up and express himself. Sean shared his sadness when his dog, Sandy, developed a tumor and had to be put down. He spoke of Danielle, a young friend who had also had her leg amputated, and had recently lost her battle with cancer. "Danielle was the same age as Sean and came into his life just as he was starting his cancer treatments. She was like an angel to him," his father says. Sean wrote to Boone about these and other losses in his young life.

It seems to me that this is one of the craziest years I have ever known. First I lost my best friend Sandy, while I was in bone marrow, or stem cell recovery. Sandy was not the most patient dog, but I loved her to death. Then just about a month ago I lost a dear friend named Danielle. I believe she saved my life in more ways than one. The same day we found out about Danielle, we got another call saying our great aunt had a brain tumor and there was no way to treat it. And now a few days ago, another person I knew passed away. I really didn't know him all that well, but it still hurts, knowing you are still here and they are in a better place.

Although much of the correspondence was poignant, there was also a lighter side. Sean thoroughly enjoyed opening his "inbox" and finding letters from his canine pen pal, as well as pictures that made him roar with laughter: Boone in his Halloween costume, Boone snowshoeing, Boone lying on his back waiting for a belly rub with all three legs pointed straight in the air.

That October, Sean and Boone had the opportunity to meet each other at a family picnic, which was sponsored by YAPS. It was held on a clear, crisp autumn day, at an equestrian center south of Denver. For the first time in over three months, Sean was able to go out in public without wearing a surgical mask, and he couldn't stop smiling. He had a wonderful time zipping between barns in a golf cart, with Boone riding beside him, his head resting on Sean's lap.

It was to be the one and only meeting. Two months later Sean passed away peacefully with his parents and sister by his side. Connie and Boone attended the funeral service; Connie sat directly behind the Flanagans, and Boone sat in the aisle beside Sean's dad, who petted him the entire time. "It was good for us. There was that 'comfort connection,'" Laura says. "Sean really loved Boone. He was a big part of his life."

After the service, as people lined up to give their condolences to the family, Boone assumed a place of honor beside the Flanagans – then he proceeded to roll over onto his back and stick his legs straight in the air. Whether Boone knew a little levity was needed, or he just wanted a good belly rub, is unknown. However, he managed to bring a smile to everyone who walked by.

Several months after the funeral, Sean's parents found a letter he had started to write to Boone, but never had a chance to mail. Sean wrote that he knew his death was imminent, and that he could accept it; he was no longer afraid. "That was a real eye-opener," Laura reveals. "You hear stories of these kids and how they know what's happening. They say certain things that, later, make you realize that they knew they were going to die. When I read that, it made me realize that Sean was an old soul."

Connie and Laura have remained in contact. Although they don't see each other often, they e-mail back and forth, confiding in each other and sharing memories. "You know how sometimes you just click with somebody?" Laura asks. "It was like that with Connie. I feel very comfortable with her. She was an important part of Sean's life and I'll always remember that."

On the fridge in the Flanagan home is the picture of Sean, riding in the golf cart alongside Boone. Connie has the same photo next to her computer.

Boone has received numerous awards for his good deeds, including being named Colorado State Therapy Assistant Dog of the Year. He was also "spokesdog" for his hometown newspaper, the *Coloradoan*, with his bright face plastered across a full-page spread. Boone continues to do "therapy work," although he now has arthritic flare-ups and uses a gurney because he can't walk down halls like he used to. And every year Boone participates in the Children's Hospital Courage Classic, a grueling 157-mile benefit bike ride to raise money for the Children's Hospital. He rides in a special trailer behind Connie's bike, which is decorated with a banner in memory of his YAPS

Sean and Boone (Photo: Laura Flanagan)

friends. "Connie and Boone keep Sean's memory alive," Laura says. "I am really thankful for that."

Things recently came full circle when Connie and Boone took a road trip. They made a detour to pay a visit to the vet who had saved Boone's life. It was a touching moment for them all. The vet was thrilled to see Boone and happy that he was doing so well. As for Connie, "I was able to express my appreciation for everything he had done for Boone, and for allowing this wonderful dog to come into my life."

Death Row Dog

Something unexpected happened one Saturday afternoon when Claire Hopkins and Willie, her flat-coated retriever cross, were making their regular visits to patients in the infirmary. An elderly man touched Willie's fur and was moved to tears. As it turns out, he had not petted a dog in 37 years.

Claire and Willie are part of a small group of volunteers who visit the infirmary at the Northern Nevada Correctional Center in Carson City, located about 35 miles south of Reno. The majority of inmates who are patients there are 60 years of age or older. Some are in wheelchairs; many suffer from a terminal disease. Most have lost contact with family and friends. The inmates don't go outside, and there are few activities to distract them from loneliness, boredom and despair. As one inmate put it, "The infirmary is where you go to die."

A visit from a friendly canine can be just what the doctor ordered. "The dogs make us feel more human," inmate Stanley Brooks says. "They allow us to feel emotions we've had buried for so many years. To have a dog look at you without judging you - that's something. Then, for the dog to lick your cheek … I'm a tough old buzzard, but that still gets to me."

Several prisons have programs where inmates train dogs, but the idea of having volunteers come into a prison infirmary to do animal-assisted activities is unique. It is largely due to the dedication and drive of Mary Harrison, a psychologist at the Correctional Center, who has a bundle of energy and an overwhelming empathy for the men she works with.

Mary volunteers at a shelter that helps find homes for abandoned animals, but it wasn't until she was visiting a friend in the hospital who was dying of pancreatic cancer, that she witnessed the healing power of animals first-hand. When a dog came into the room, her friend's face would light up, and for the duration of the dog's visit he laughed, petted the dog and seemed able to put aside his problems and pain.

"The effect was so profound that Mary wondered if there was a way she could implement a similar program for the inmates she affectionately refers to as "the old guys." She approached Claire, a fellow volunteer at the shelter who was already active in animal-assisted activities. The two brainstormed, and Mary put together a proposal that was presented to the warden and prison director. They quickly got on board, although not everyone at the prison was enthused. According to Claire, some of the correctional officers thought it was too "touchy-feely."

All of the volunteers go through a special orientation class to learn the protocols of volunteering at the prison, such as not mailing letters for the inmates, not bringing anything into the prison, and not giving out personal information. It is also important that visitors don't wear the same colors as the inmates, so that correctional officers can easily differentiate between them if there is an emergency.

Still, as prepared as the volunteers were, Claire admits that the first visit to the facility was surreal. The infirmary is at the far end of the prison complex. She and Willie had to walk through an armored gate, and across a yard surrounded by barbed wire and a chain-link fence. There were double doors, armed towers and slamming gates.

But any fears she had quickly subsided. The men were extremely respectful of the volunteers. They were grateful that someone was taking a genuine interest in them, and they loved their new "canine therapists." As for Willie, he was an immediate hit. Claire proudly describes him as "extremely friendly with a laid-back personality. He falls in love with everyone he meets." He worked the room like a pro, doling out healthy doses of unconditional love in return for a pat or a scratch on the back.

The volunteers' duties expanded the following year, when Mary created a structured living program for the general prison inmate population. She felt it was important to motivate the men, most of whom are geriatric, and "get them out of their beds in the morning" in order to increase their physical and mental health. The program includes exercise, crafts, addiction support groups and games such as wheelchair basketball and softball (which are high-spirited, competitive and not for the faint-of-heart). In keeping with her goal of including animal-assisted therapy, Mary arranged for Claire, Willie, and the other volunteers to visit these men as well.

The inmates were directly involved in planning the new program, and wanted it to have a catchy name. After much discussion they settled on "True Grit." Since one of their first special activities was a visit from Willie, they decided he should appear on their logo, alongside a man in a wheelchair. Willie wore a patch over one eye, a tribute to John Wayne in the movie "True Grit."

Willie has another qualification for his mascot role: He's an "ex-con" himself. Claire rescued him from a high-kill shelter when he was only six months old. This resonates deeply with the prison inmates. They liked the idea that Willie, whose only "crime" was that nobody wanted him, had been saved, and gave him the moniker "Death Row Dog."

Stanley wrote a special song for Willie and asked for permission to bring his guitar into the infirmary to sing it. When he did, there was not a dry eye in the room.

Willie (Photo: Claire Hopkins)

Death Row Dog

I'd like to tell you about my friend
That I occasionally get to see
He hardly ever has a word to say
But he means a lot to me.
Willie comes to see us every month or so
Just to bring a little cheer
And he's got the toughest, most macho of us
Fighting hard to hide a salty tear.

I understand he was adopted
Just when they were ready to put him down
And when I feel the love that Willie brings to us
I'm sure glad that he's still around.

It's sorta like the kind of love
That fills a mother's heart
A love that's there even when you're wrong
Because it's been there from the start.

When he lets you pet him or hug him
Or when he licks your hand or face
Willie tells you he's not judging you
For being here in this place.
See, he was locked up once himself
And now that he is free
He spends his time bringing hope and love
To folks like you and me.

He only wants to let us know
Though the world may turn a deaf ear
That once a month, for an hour or so
Willie shows us he really cares.
Yes, I'd like to tell you all about my friend
But the right words just seem to flee
So come on back Willie, every chance you get
Because we love you too, you see.

Stanley W. Brooks

Like Claire, volunteer Polly Sarfield has been with the program from the start. Polly, a second-grade English as a Second Language (ESL) teacher, says the impact of the dogs is very powerful. "The men sit in a circle, patiently waiting to chat with us and to pet and hug the dogs. They're ever so polite; they're real gentlemen." The men converse about a variety of subjects and are very interested – and interesting. "They also talk about their own dogs that they had to leave behind, and sometimes even go back to their rooms to get pictures of them. They truly miss them; it's easy to see that."

Polly first started visiting alongside her Leonberger named Brendan. "Leos" are a large, friendly breed with thick brown fur and a black mask. About a year after the program began, Brendan was diagnosed with cancer and had to undergo surgery to have his hind a leg removed. Out of necessity, he took a two-month break. Polly says that the inmates were incredibly caring and concerned about Brendan, constantly sending him their good wishes and inquiring about him.

When Brendan was well enough to return to the prison, he was given a hero's welcome. The inmates were clearly inspired, and many were able to relate to him in a new and deeply personal way. Several suffered severe illness; some had undergone chemotherapy. A higher-

Brendan and Inmate (Photo: Mary Harrison)

than-average number of inmates have amputations as a result of war, diabetes or gunshot wounds.

Polly and Brendan continued to visit for several months. "As long as he was strong enough to maintain balance, we came," Polly says. Unfortunately, the cancer spread to Brendan's lungs and shortly thereafter, he succumbed to the disease.

His death had a profound impact on the inmates. As one of them put it, "Brendan was one of the mellowest and noble fellows I ever met. The first visit after his surgery was a moving experience. He was so happy to see all of us. When he passed away it felt like a friend had died."

The inmates mourned Brendan's passing, and many confessed to Polly that they cried upon learning of his death, and said prayers and rosaries for him. They made a bouquet of roses out of paper and presented it to Polly, along with a signed card. It was their way of saying goodbye, and thank you, for all he had meant to them.

Polly now volunteers with Rusty, a Leonberger who was rescued when he was eight years old. Before that, Rusty seemed to have the perfect existence. He lived in North Carolina and was part of a large family that had four kids. He would attend all their soccer games and go everywhere with them. "Then something happened," Polly says. "I don't know what. Perhaps it was a nasty divorce or something like that, but Rusty was abandoned and left outside to fend for himself. The family simply moved away. Rusty wandered the streets begging for food, water and safety, before someone finally called the Leonberger rescue group." The Leonberger community is very small and as it turned out, Rusty was the litter-mate of the first "Leo" Polly had owned. Needless to say, she adopted him on the spot.

Polly tells me that the visits to the prison have been one of the most rewarding experiences of her life. "Some people around here don't believe in what we are doing," she says. "They feel that because the prisoners committed crimes, they deserve what they got and certainly don't deserve anything else." Polly believes those critics should take a lesson from the dogs. "They give unconditional love; they don't care about what you've done in the past. What's important is how you treat them now."

The canine visitors clearly fuel compassion and generosity among the inmates. Mary asked the inmates to fill out a questionnaire regarding the impact of the dogs. Some mentioned the lessons they learned from their canine friends. "Dogs instill values like loyalty, friendship and compassion," one inmate wrote. "I'm learning how to get along with other people," reported another. "It changes my opinion of people. It makes me realize that people on the outside do care."

Some inmates cite how a visit from the dogs takes away stress and turmoil. "It mellows me out just to be around them. It is one of the few moments you can show affection to something around here." One inmate mentioned the lighter side of the program: "The best part is watching how the other men enjoy the dogs. There's something about dogs that brings out the little kid in people. It's fun (and even a little bit funny) to watch a bunch of old men behave like kids."

Willie and Inmate (Photo: Mary Harrison)

The first Christmas of the program, the inmates presented each dog with a latch-hooked rug they had made. The rugs were decorated with the dog's name, and a picture of either a paw print or a bone. They had also made a special one that said, "In memory of Brendan."

"The men were ever so kind," Polly says, clearly touched. "Oh my gosh! You think of prison as having these big, burly guys who are hardened and tough. And lo and behold, they do something like that."

Claire echoes this sentiment. When she made the decision to retire Willie last Christmas because he is getting on in years, she was deeply moved by the inmates' response. They requested special permission to host a combination Christmas/retirement party. The warden presented Claire and Willie with a plaque to thank them for their service, and one of the inmates crafted some homemade flowers and presented them together with a card. The words written on the card were a generic greeting:

Wishing you a truly joyous Christmas and a very Happy New Year.

Below, the prisoner had signed his name and then wrote:

Silent amends.
Every opportunity I get to do something nice for someone, peels back another thin layer
of the guilt that I feel for harming someone.

The "big, burly guys" in the Northern Nevada Correctional Center are resigned to "doing their time." They know they have a debt to society, which they are prepared to pay. Most of them will die in prison, far away from loved ones and friends. But not before they have come to know the healing power of a four-legged furry friend.

Dobie

One fine spring day in June, 2005, Duane Hodges was driving his car out of a four-story parking garage. All of a sudden he glimpsed a movement out of the corner of his eye. Turning, he saw a tiny black Labrador retriever puppy, about three or four months old, crawling out onto the lawn next to the parking ramp.

Duane immediately pulled over and got out of his car to take a closer look. The pup was pitifully thin, with ribs clearly visible through his skin. He crawled forward and tried to stand up, but his back legs could not support his weight. He was obviously hungry and needed help. And, much to Duane's amazement, the little puppy was wagging his tail.

Just then animal control arrived. It seemed that someone else had seen the injured puppy and given them a call. An officer told Duane that because the puppy was injured, it would probably have to be put to sleep. Duane balked at the idea and gave the officers his phone number, saying if no one came forward to claim the puppy they should contact him.

Duane, who was raised on ranches in Montana and Wyoming, has had an undying love of animals all his life. However, due to personal circumstances, it was impossible for him to take care of a dog on his own. Fortunately, Duane's very good friend, Richard Bartel, was in a position to help.

Dobie as a puppy (Photo: Richard Bartel)

When Richard, a fellow animal-lover, heard about the injured dog, he was deeply moved. That night, he found it difficult to sleep. "I realized I was thinking about the puppy, so I said a prayer for it, then finally drifted off," Richard says. "The next morning, I woke up with a voice running through my brain that was saying, 'Help the puppy.'"

Forty-eight hours after finding the dog, Duane got a call. Because of the extent of the pup's injuries, he was being held at the veterinary clinic instead of the pound. No one had come forward to claim him, so Duane was asked if he would be willing to come to the clinic the next morning to authorize treatment. Otherwise the pup would have to be euthanized; there was no one else they could contact.

Duane asked Richard if he would accompany him to the clinic. Richard, who works in hospital maintenance, has flexible hours and is able to take time off during the week, so he readily agreed. And knowing Duane was not in a financial position to take on veterinary expenses, he dusted off his VISA card.

Richard and Duane arrived at the clinic early the next morning, and were sitting in the waiting room when they heard a rustling sound. Then the little puppy came down the hall. He had been given painkillers and was hobbling towards them, even though his back legs were broken. "The puppy just ran up to me," Duane says, "and that kinda broke my heart."

The puppy was just skin and bones, but so full of life. The staff said that he had almost certainly belonged to someone. He was used to being around people and had already learned some commands. He would *sit* on command, he knew the word *no*, and when he went outside and was told *go potty*, he would do so.

The vet felt that x-rays were needed to determine the extent of the injuries. When the results came back, they were sobering: both thigh bones had been shattered at the point where the legs connect with the pelvis. The vet explained that this type of injury could not have occurred if the pup had been hit by a car, or had jumped or fallen off the parking garage. Instead, someone must have held the little pup by his armpits, and then let him drop four stories, where he landed squarely on his buttocks on the pavement below. The injuries appeared to have been over 10 days old, and the vet speculated that the pup had been outside, with no food and only rainwater to drink, for the entire time.

After doing what she could to make the pup comfortable, the vet handed Richard an envelope containing the x-rays, and suggested making an appointment at the University of Minnesota Veterinary Teaching Hospital.

Richard was familiar with the university. He had attended it as a student, and remembered walking across campus on his way to classes. Off to one side was a statue that resembled the one in the TV sitcom, "The Many Loves of Dobie Gillis," where a teenaged Dobie (Dwayne Hickman) and his friends would sit and discuss the meaning of life. Since the little pup was going to be attending the university as well, Richard thought the name "Dobie" would be a perfect fit.

Richard brought Dobie home and introduced him to his 12-year-old dog, Gabby, who he jokingly refers to as a basset/ "terrorist" mix. Richard wasn't sure how Gabby would react to no longer being an "only dog," but after an initial period of aloofness, a few extra treats and some obedience training, she warmed up. The two have since become good friends.

An appointment was made at the university for the following day. The next morning, just as Richard was getting ready to leave, he received a telephone call from the University of Minnesota's media relations department. One of Duane's co-workers had e-mailed WCCO Television, a local station affiliated with CBS, and told them about the injured dog. The station wanted to do a story on Dobie, and if Richard agreed, would send a camera crew to meet them at the hospital.

Richard realized that having the media cover Dobie's story was a good opportunity to publicize animal abuse. He agreed, but because he wanted the story to focus on the pup, opted to stay in the examining room while the segment was being taped. And Duane agreed to be interviewed at the foot of the parking garage where Dobie had been found.

Veterinarian specialists at the university hospital said that Dobie would need a double femoral head ostectomy. This surgical procedure would remove the shattered knuckle-like parts of the femur (leg) bones, which fit into the groove of the hips. Because Dobie was so young artificial joints were not an option, they explained. However, fibrous scar tissue and muscle would develop, filling in the space and creating "false" hip joints where the femoral heads had been. After the surgery he would require extensive rehabilitation therapy.

The day before Dobie underwent surgery his story aired on the six o'clock news, and the station was inundated with calls and e-mails from people wanting to donate to the little pup's care. Duane's co-worker Jill Kaspszak, and her husband Paul, set up the "Dobie Fund" which routed donations to the University of Minnesota Foundation, to be earmarked for the pup's medical expenses. Local country and western artist Bo Billy put on a benefit concert at a local pub. A newspaper ran a story about the fundraising efforts, and in response two wealthy and generous individuals contacted the university and matched donations – not only to the Dobie Fund, but to several other fundraising efforts there. One person's cruelty lead to so many people banding together that in the end a staggering $90,000 had been raised. That was more than enough to cover Dobie's medical treatment, and remaining funds were donated to the Foundation for the care of abused animals.

Despite having undergone major surgery Dobie was still able to walk. He could shift much of his weight onto his front legs, while his rear legs and pelvis were supported by thigh muscle mass. Lin Gelbman, Certified Canine Rehab Practitioner and Coordinator for Rehabilitation at the University of Minnesota College of Veterinarian Medicine, says that animals are often able to compensate this way. However, this can result in an uneven gait, as well as problems such as front elbow and shoulder pain. Guided rehabilitation would be needed to teach Dobie to distribute his weight evenly and, because he was still a puppy, to build muscle mass in his rear legs to support him as he continued to grow.

Lin worked with Dobie for almost a year. Part of his rehabilitation involved using an underwater treadmill – a device that resembles a large aquarium and is filled with water that is at a therapeutic temperature, similar to a spa. Walking on the treadmill is a low-impact form of exercise designed to increase strength and mobility, without stress on the joints.

At home, Richard exercised Dobie by taking him to the backyard and throwing twigs short distances for him to fetch. One day, about a month after starting therapy, Dobie disappeared around the side of the house. When he came back he was carrying an entire branch in his mouth! For Richard, "That was the moemnt when I knew that everything was going to be alright." "Dogs are amazing, they truly are," Lin says. As for Richard, he remembers thinking, "Everything is going to be all right."

"Animals love rehab," Lin says, and Dobie was no exception. "He was such a little guy when he started, but he was always 'Mr. Happy.' He was such a champ." Dobie was also very clever. He figured out how to get all four feet onto the side panel of the treadmill, or on the front panel, so he didn't have to walk! Lin has worked with animals for over 30 years, and has been at the rehab center for six, and Dobie is the first dog who has managed to do that. "It was pretty cute," she has to admit, even though it meant getting into the tank with him to rearrange his feet.

As soon as it was feasible, Lin recommended that, in addition to three-times-a-week therapy sessions, Dobie attend obedience class. This would increase his level of cooperation during his rehabilitation (and result in less underwater immersions for her). Lin, who is also a trainer, suggested enrolling Dobie in the school where she worked. That way she could liaise with the other trainers, and explain Dobie's physical limitations so that they could be accommodated.

Dobie excelled in his obedience classes, and as a result his rehab sessions progressed more smoothly. But he still maintained a playful streak. For example, Lin has a pair of water wings – the kind that kids use in swimming pools to keep afloat – which she will sometimes put on an animal's legs, to increase resistance while they are walking on the underwater treadmill. They are brightly colored, with a picture of the cartoon character Sponge Bob on them. When Lin tried putting these on Dobie, he was not impressed. "He kept trying to bite them off," she says with a laugh. "Well, I certainly had to correct that! I kept saying, 'No Dobie, you cannot eat Mr. Sponge Bob Squarepants!'"

As Dobie's rehab progressed, Lin set up a schedule of exercises to be done at home every day. Richard was chief "coach" and Daune acted as "backup trainer" if his friend was away. The exercises included walking over elevated bars, leg lifts where he would stand on one rear leg while the other one was held in the air, and moving from *sit* to *stand,* which builds quadriceps strength. Richard also took Dobie on daily walks, with very specific instructions, such as climbing a hill in a zigzag pattern to increase muscle and control Dobie's side-to-side mobility.

By the time Dobie was discharged from rehab, all the hard work had paid off. "He can run and play with the best of them," Lin says.

"Not having hip joints doesn't affect him one way or the other." Dobie's rear end is about two inches shorter than normal, and his gait is slightly different than other Labs, but it is hardly noticeable.

Richard continued to take Dobie to obedience classes, where he met an instructor who was a member of Therapy Dogs International (TDI®). Started in 1976, TDI has approximately 20,000 dog/handler teams who visit in hospitals, schools, senior homes and other facilities. The group operates in a similar manner to Delta Society®, but rather than use the term "animal-assisted activities," they refer to their canine members as Therapy Dogs. "We feel the term 'animal-assisted' is not technically correct," President Ursula Kempe explains. "Our dogs are the therapists and we are only the handlers. The magic happens between the dog and the person being seen."

Richard realized that Dobie, with his gentle demeanor and his love of people, was a good candidate for a therapy dog. "It just seemed to make sense. Dobie was so socialized, and he gets his energy from being around people," Richard says. "Many people gave a lot of encouragement and support to get him here, and it's just a way to thank them, by letting him help someone else."

Passing the TDI test required more training. Dobie was still a puppy, so he tended to be rambunctious and easily distracted, especially if food was involved. But he was always good-natured and eager to please. Richard clearly remembers the day he knew Dobie was ready to be a therapy dog. "Our class was held in an old dance hall and our instructor had set up an obstacle course of sorts. Then she scattered stuffed toys, empty plastic bottles, empty food wrappers, and a big dish of kibble throughout the room. I had to put Dobie in a *sit* in one corner of the room and then cross diagonally to the opposite corner and command Dobie to *come*. I gave the command and this beautiful black dog pranced right past that entire room filled with temptation and sat at my side."

Once Dobie passed the test and was certified, Richard started to look around for a place to volunteer. He joined Pals on Paws Chapter 125, a local group affiliated with Therapy Dog International. Many TDI teams visit in local hospitals, but since Richard worked in one, he felt he wanted to begin with a challenge of a different sort. Richard's friend, Bonnie Sykora, is program director at Phoenix Alternative Inc., a day program for adults with severe disabilities such as cerebral palsy, head injuries and autism. He phoned and asked if she knew of any facilities that were looking for a therapy dog.

As it happened, Bonnie was just in the process of looking for the phone number for TDI. "We'd been wanting a therapy dog *forever*, but were having difficulty finding someone because we're only open during the day and most people aren't available then," Bonnie says. "The call from Richard was truly heaven sent."

Phoenix Alternative Inc. is located in White Bear Lake, Minnesota. The clients, aged 18 and older, have severe mental, physical and medical challenges. They are brought to the center during the day to participate in recreational, leisure and community events, as well as adaptive skill development. There are seven different areas, similar to classrooms, where clients are placed with teachers and staff according to their interests, abilities and skills. This was just the sort of opportunity Richard was looking for, and soon after the conversation with Bonnie, he and Dobie started to volunteer.

Dobie's impact was felt immediately. A very gentle, calm and loving dog, he brightens the day simply by walking into a room. "It's amazing how in tune he is," Bonnie says. "Life doesn't always give our clients a lot of opportunity. Then you see them petting Dobie, and that sense of weariness just seems to go away."

Some of the clients in the program are higher functioning, and are able to recall pets they have had in the past. Those in wheelchairs wait for Dobie to come up to them and snuggle as close as he can get. Some can pet Dobie with their hands; others have difficulty reaching down to his level, so the staff will take off their shoes and the clients will

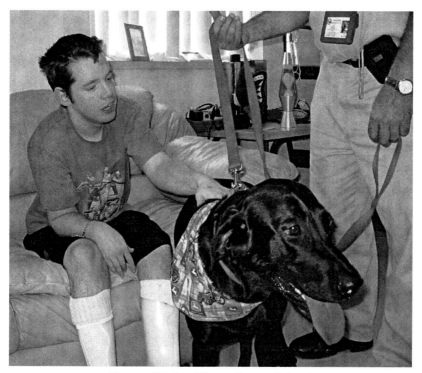

Tony and Dobie (Photo: Bonnie Sykora)

rub his ears with their feet. "Many of our clients have lost the feeling in their hands and their feet because they don't move, touch and feel. Dobie is very soft, and petting and touching him is not only fun and interesting, it stimulates and alerts the brain in different ways."

One client, named Tony, had very basic communication skills and difficulty engaging in conversation that was appropriate to the event taking place. Richard recalls their first meeting, and Tony's subsequent progress. "I noticed a young man walking towards us. His eyes were as big as saucers, and there was a huge smile on his face. He slowly reached down, touched Dobie's fur, and started saying 'Woof, woof.' The staff helped coax a couple of words out of him and soon he started saying, 'Nice puppy, woof, woof.'"

Within a few months, Tony's vocabulary had expanded and he began to express himself more. "He would pat his canine therapist and say, 'Nice Dobie,'" Richard says. "Then he would tease me by putting his hand on my shoulder and saying 'Nice kitty!' He always noticed when I wore a red shirt – his favorite color – and would say 'Nice shirt!'"

Richard describes Tony as a "very special, very tender young man, who loved to greet you, and joke with you. He especially loved to come up to you and say 'knock, knock.' He would then laugh and laugh. He never knew any punchlines, but 'knock knock' was funny enough for him." And he was always delighted when Dobie would go over to sit beside him, and hang out for awhile.

Tony passed away at age 30, just as this book was going to press. His mother recalls the special connection he shared with his four-legged friend. "Dobie enriched Tony's life," she says. "He greatly enjoyed petting Dobie and saying 'Good Dobie.' That connection had love, joy and comfort in it."

Another memorable experience for Richard was meeting and working with Sandra, a client who has Rett Syndrome, a neurological disorder that occurs almost exclusively in females. Those with Rett Syndrome have limited language skills, and the inability to perform motor functions including purposeful hand moments such as grasping, reaching and touching things.

Sandra has been coming to the center for nine years. Except for the times when the staff assists her in using her hands functionally, she sits in her chair with her fists tightly clenched. The first time that she saw Dobie her eyes opened wide, so Richard brought Dobie up to her as close as he could. The same thing occurred the following week. On the third visit, with the staff's help, Sandra slowly unclenched her clasped hands. Then, much to the surprise of everyone, she reached out and began to pet Dobie by herself.

The staff relishes the opportunity to pet and dote on Dobie as well, and he is more than willing to oblige. After two years and over

100 visits, as Richard puts it, "He kind of thinks he owns the place now." His photo is on the desk in the reception area, and he knows where all the treats are kept. He even goes into Bonnie's office and pokes his nose at the drawer, until she opens it and gives him a reward.

Bonnie has nothing but praise for the visiting team. "Richard and Dobie have an incredible bond," she says. "It's really the partnership between them that makes it such a success." Richard, however, sees it another way. "I truly believe that it has been God and Dobie doing the work. I'm just grateful to be able to stand on the sidelines and watch them work their miracles together."

Aside from their weekly visits to Phoenix Alternatives, Richard and Dobie visit in nursing homes and help distribute information about animal therapy at pet expos and the renaissance fair. They even go to the University of Minnesota Law School during the final week of classes to help students de-stress as they prepare for their exams. Once again Richard is modest about his contribution, saying "Dobie does the work; I drive the car."

Dobie's rehabilitation involved a huge commitment of time and energy, as well as money. "I know there are people that question whether saving a dog's life is worth thousands of dollars," Richard says. "Thankfully, there were many people who generously donated money to the University of Minnesota to offset the cost of Dobie's care. I want everyone to know that it was worth it, and was greatly appreciated."

These days Dobie is one happy, active dog. He loves swimming, tennis balls and food of any kind. Richard strives to keep Dobie's weight in check so not to add extra stress on his joints, with a controlled diet and 45-minute walks zigzagging up and down hills. While getting up every morning to exercise, rain or shine, can be difficult, there have been a few unexpected side benefits. Richard's blood pressure is down and his cholesterol is lower. Not only that, but he has lost 60 pounds.

Richard makes a point of periodically dropping by the rehab center to visit. Dobie is always very excited to see everyone who worked

Richard and Dobie (Photo: Courtesy of Phoenix Alternates Inc.)

with him, and can hardly wait to get in the room. And if the door
to the underwater treadmill is open, he'll run right over and jump
inside the tank. Then he'll stand there while Richard and Lin catch
up, with a look as if to say, "Come on you guys, when is the fun going to start?"

PART FOUR

Resources

Information on Adopting a Dog

Adopting a dog should never be a spur-of-the-moment decision. A dog may be with you for 15 years or more. It is important to take the time and make sure that you are ready to welcome a special friend into your life, that you are aware of the costs involved and that you choose the dog that will be a good match for you.

Dogs require exercise, veterinary care, companionship, feeding, training and plenty of love, as well as a significant amount of time and energy. All dogs require grooming, but some breeds may need more than others, and the cost of a professional groomer may need to be added into the budget. And don't forget toys!

Not all types of dogs are suited to every individual. Puppies require more time and attention, as well as training, and of course patience when it comes to the inevitable "accidents" and chewed prized possessions. Big dogs do not always require more exercise than smaller dogs, but they do need more space. Some dogs are more suited to families with children, or those who already have another pet in the home.

The following resources are helpful both before, and after, adopting a pet.

Websites
The American Society for the Prevention of Cruelty to Animals (ASPCA®)

www.aspca.org

Founded in 1866, the ASPCA was the first humane organization in the western hemisphere. Their website provides tips that include "Questions to Ask Yourself Before Adopting," and "Top 10 Things To Do Before You Bring Your New Dog Home," as well as information on pet overpopulation and how to help or start a shelter. There is also a searchable database to find shelters in your area.

The Humane Society of the United States

www.humanesociety.org

The nation's largest animal protection organization, their website provides information on how to choose the pet that's right for you and your family, and includes links to popular adoption websites. They also provide information and solutions for allergies, behavior-related issues and renting with pets.

American Humane Association (AHA)

www.americanhumane.org

The AHA is an umbrella group for member animal shelters. Their website contains information on the problem of pet overpopulation, pet adoption, behavior, training and care.

Also, all of the websites listed under Internet Pet Adoption Sites (page 199) provide valuable information on pet adoption.

Books

Your Adopted Dog: Everything You Need to Know about Rescuing and Caring for a Best Friend in Need. Shelley Frost and Katerina Lorenzatos Makris, The Lyons Press; 1st edition (September 1, 2007).

Petfinder.com – The Adopted Dog Bible (Your One-Stop Resource for Choosing, Training and Caring for Your Sheltered or Rescued Dog). Kim Saunders, Harper Paperbacks (January 20, 2009).

Finding the
Perfect Shelter Dog

There are several ways to begin your search for the perfect dog – through animal shelters, rescue organizations, breed rescues, or Internet adoption websites.

The aim of every rescue and shelter is to find an appropriate, loving home for an animal, where they will be able to remain for the rest of their life. Most shelters and rescues will ask for a donation and/or an adoption fee to help cover a portion of their expenses. These may include immunizations, a microchip for identification should the animal become separated from its home, food and shelter, and the cost of spaying or neutering. If the animal has been injured or abused, the shelter may incur additional medical expenses to bring the dog's health up to a level where adoption is possible.

Finding the perfect match may take time, but it is definitely worth it. You will be rewarded with love, licks and the type of unconditional love that only a dog can provide.

Animal Shelters

Animal shelters take in stray and homeless animals, providing temporary shelter until the animals are reclaimed by their owner, adopted out, or placed with other organizations. Many shelters also provide low cost spaying and neutering, vaccinations and other veterinary services, and educational resources for pet owners.

Due to limited space and financial resources, and the overwhelming number of homeless animals, many shelters are only able to provide housing for animals for a limited period of time, after which the animals are euthanized. Others have a "no kill" policy, which means animals are only euthanized when they are too sick to be treated, too aggressive for adoption, or are in severe distress.

Shelters have a large variety of dogs of all ages; an estimated 20 to 25% are purebred dogs. In fact, they may have just the pet you are looking for.

Some shelters are private, non-profit entities; others are run by local municipalites. They can usually be found in the Yellow Pages™ where they may be listed under "animal control," "humane society," or "animal shelter."

Other ways to locate shelters are through the Shelter Pet Project (www.theshelterpetproject.com), Internet pet adoption websites (page 200), or the ASPCA's "Find a Shelter Database." (www.aspca.org/adoption/shelters)

Rescue Organizations

Rescue groups are run by volunteers, and may vary in size from a large group of people to a single, dedicated individual. They often obtain animals from the local shelters, and sometimes help to transport animals from locations where there are a high number of homeless pets, like in the aftermath of Hurricane Katrina. There are also rescues dedicated to re-homing specific breeds (see below).

Unlike shelters, most rescue groups do not have a "brick and mortar" structure. The animals are fostered in private homes, which enable them to be held until they are adopted out. The groups spend a significant amount of time and effort evaluating a dog. They provide the necessary veterinary care, as well as re-socializing and retraining prior to adoption. Potential adopters are thoroughly screened and home visits are usually mandatory. Animals are not generally euthanized, except in the case of severe medical or behavioral problems.

Adoption fees vary, depending on veterinary and other costs that have been incurred. These fees rarely cover expenses and most rescue groups dig deep into their own pockets to provide shelter and care for their dogs. Unfortunately, many groups cannot keep up with the numbers of dogs in need of their assistance and must turn down dogs when their foster homes are full.

One of the best ways to locate rescue groups is via the Internet ("animal rescue" + location). Some groups hold adoption events at stores such as PETCO® and PetSmart®, where available animals are brought for a meet-and-greet with potential adopters. Many shelters and rescues also have links and information posted on Internet pet adoption sites (page 200).

Breed Rescues

Due to the increasing number of homeless dogs, there are now rescue groups dedicated to re-homing almost every imaginable breed of dog. They are run by dedicated volunteers with a wealth of knowledge and a deep love for a specific breed. These volunteers work hard to make sure that potential adopters have a thorough understanding of the traits of the breed and know what to expect when adopting a dog. They also provide counseling and follow-up advice.

Breed rescue groups often get animals from shelters, veterinary hospitals or kennels if a pet has been abandoned there, and from owners who, due to medical or economic reasons, are no longer able to take care of their dogs.

One way to locate these rescues is by doing an Internet search (for example, "Labrador retriever" + "rescue"), which will probably turn up a variety of contacts per breed. As well, many purebred dog clubs run their own rescue groups and can be found by searching on-line (for example, "Labrador retriever club" + "rescue"). The American Kennel Club also provides links to hundreds of purebred rescue groups (www.akc.org/breeds.rescue.cfm).

Internet Pet Adoption Sites

Internet matchmaking for those looking for love (at least of the furry, four-legged kind)! The following websites provide a database for searching for adoptable animals. The search engines let you enter location according to zip code, as well as type of animal (mostly dogs and cats, but horses, rabbits, reptiles and birds, as well), breed, age, sex and size. Search results display photographs of the animals, as well as personality profile, health information, and links to the rescue or shelter group where the pet is staying.

Shelters and rescue groups are responsible for updating their information, and may post information on more than one website. Each has its own criteria for adoption and applications are made directly through the groups themselves. Adoption fees may vary as well.

Some shelter and rescue groups credit up to 50 percent of their adoptions to Internet pet adoption sites. This is due to a number of factors. People may be reticent to visit a shelter in person, fearing it will be too traumatic or that they will make an impulsive choice. These "virtual shelters" allow you to take your time and gather information about prospective pets. They provide access to thousands of shelters and rescues, including smaller ones and those that don't have a physical space, but use foster homes. The sites are also free, and easy to use. Many provide invaluable additional resources as well.

Adopt-a-Pet

www.AdoptaPet.com
1-800-Save-A-Pet.com (1-800-728-3273)
info@AdoptaPet.com
Adopt-a-Pet links over 8,000 shelters and rescue groups from across the United States with potential adopters. Sponsored by Purina®, it also powers searches for other high-traffic sites such as PetSmart.com and MarthaStewart.com.

Petfinder.com
www.Petfinder.com
This database links information on more than 300,000 profiles of homeless pets and almost 12,000 non-profit animal welfare groups, both in Canada and the United States. The site is enormously successful and has been responsible for almost 12 million pet adoptions so far!

PETS911
www.Pets911.com
This site has listings for thousands of animals from over 9,600 member shelters and rescue organizations nationwide.

Shelter Pet Project
ww.theshelterpetproject.org

In Canada:
Adopt an Animal
www.Adoptananimal.ca
This database provides links to over 900 rescue, adoption, shelter and sanctuary organizations, as well as purebred rescues operating across Canada, searchable by province and postal code.

Canada's Guide to Dogs
www.canadasguidetodogs.com/rescue.htm
This website provides a list of rescue organizations and shelters, searchable by province.

In Great Britain:
Dogpages
www.dogpages.org.uk
Over 1,000 rescues and shelters throughout the United Kingdom and Ireland are included on this site, searchable by region. There is also a separate section to search for rescue groups according to breed.

Ways You Can Help

Spay or Neuter Your Pet

Between three and four million cats and dogs are euthanized each year in the US alone. Help prevent overpopulation and unwanted litters by spaying or neutering your pet. The American Society for the Prevention of Cruelty to Animals (ASPCA) website offers a searchable database of low-cost spay/neuter programs: www.aspca.org/petcare/spayneuter. *In Canada, many local shelters offer low-cost spay and neuter clinics periodically throughout the year. Call your local Humane Society, SPCA, or shelter for more information.*

Proper Identification

An estimated one in three pets will become lost at some point during their lifetime. The majority are never reunited with their owners. It is estimated that without proper identification, only two percent of lost cats and 17 percent of dogs are returned home. Millions more are euthanized annually because their owners could not be located. The ASPCA strongly suggests that you licence your pet. Licenses, which must be renewed annually, contain information that can be used to track down owners. The ASPCA also recommends that your pet have a microchip and a proper ID tag.

Microchips about the size of a grain of rice are implanted under the skin of your pet. They contain information about a contact agency, which maintains a database of owner information, and can be read by a scanner.

It is now standard practice for veterinary offices and shelters to check lost pets for microchips. Implanting the microchip is virtually pain free, provides a permanent form of identification, and is inexpensive – a one-time fee of anywhere from $20 to $50. It is important to note that not all microchips can be read by all scanners, so it is a good idea to request one that is compatible with the scanners that are most commonly used.

Contact your Local Shelter or Rescue Organization

Shelters and animal rescue organizations are always struggling to find funding and volunteers. There are many ways to help animals in need. For example:

- Donate Money - A monetary donation is always welcome; some organizations encourage you to commit to a small monthly sum, rather than a one-time donation. Regular donations, no matter how small, help an organization plan for the future, rather than having to guess what their future budget will be like. Contact your local shelter, rescue organization or Humane Society.

- Donate Time – Whether you walk dogs, stuff envelopes, assist with fundraising, or simply spend time helping with upkeep, volunteering at a local shelter or rescue organization is one hands-on way to make a contribution to helping animals in desperate need.

- Donate Goods – Gifts of leashes, blankets, toys and food are always gratefully received. If you are considering a gift of this sort, a quick call to your local shelter or rescue will give you a good idea of what sorts of things they are in need of.

- Foster an Abandoned Animal – Many rescue groups are forced to turn away animals in desperate straits if their foster homes are full. Fostering an animal not only helps keep them safe until an appropriate home can be found, but is extremely rewarding for those who provide the foster care.

Volunteer with Your Dog

Many organizations provide testing, accreditation, support and training for those wishing to volunteer with their pets. Delta Society®, Therapy Dogs Inc. and Therapy Dogs International (TDI®) have members in all 50 states, as well as in Canada and other countries.

Delta Society

www.deltasociety.org

Delta Society has over 10,000 registered Pet Partners® teams in the United States, as well as Canada, Mexico, India, Japan, Korea and Sweden. The R.E.A.D.® (Reading Educational Assistance Dogs) is a trademarked program with Intermountain Therapy Animals (www. therapyanimals.org), which is affiliated with Delta Society.

Therapy Dogs Inc.

www.therapydogs.com

Therapy Dogs Inc. has almost 12,000 members, with branches in the United States, Canada and Puerto Rico.

Therapy Dogs International (TDI®)

www.tdi-dog.org

tdi@gti.net

The oldest and largest of the organizations, TDI has approximately 20,000 dog/handler teams in the United States and Canada. They also have a Tail Waggin' Tutors program, where children read to dogs.

There are numerous smaller groups all across the United States, as well as in Canada, Australia and the United Kingdom. A complete list can be found on the website Dogplay, which is dedicated to encouraging a higher level of interaction between people and their dogs (www.dogplay.com/Activities/Therapy/index.html). The site also has a wealth of information including how to start your own program, as well as books, articles and networking links.

Click to Give

The easiest possible way to make a difference and help those in need – at no cost to you and in only a few seconds a day. Simply go to the Animal Rescue Site™ (www.theanimalrescuesite.com) and click on the purple "Click to Give"button. For each click, the site's sponsors donate food to animals in need. Purchases made via the online store provide additional food and animal care. In 2008, visitor clicks funded over 67 million bowls of food to needy animals, and almost 11 million bowls of food were funded through purchases via the store.

The Animal Rescue Site is part of the GreaterGood.com™ network of Click to Give sites which allow you to donate to causes such as breast cancer, world hunger, child health, rainforest protection and child literacy. One hundred percent of sponsorship advertising goes to charitable partners.

Organizations

4 Paws for Ability
www.4pawsforability.org
253 Dayton Ave.
Xenia, OH 45385
Phone: 937-374-0385

Training Center:
207 Dayton Ave.
Xenia, OH 45385
Phone: 937-376-2781

Amazing Tails, LLC, Inc.
www.amazing-service-dogs.com
651 Scroggy Rd.
Oxford, PA 19363
Phone: 717-529-6875

American Humane Society
63 Inverness Dr. E.
Englewood, CO 80112
Phone: 303-792-9900
Toll-free: 1-800-227-4645
www.americanhumane.org

American Kennel Club (AKC)
www.akc.org

**American Kennel Club's Canine
Good Citizen®** (CGC) Program
www.akc.org/events/cgc

**American Society for the Prevention
of Cruelty to Animals** (ASPCA®)
424 East 92nd St.
New York, NY 10128-6804
Phone: 212-876-7700
www.aspca.org

**American Temperament Test Society,
Inc.** (ATTS)
P.O. Box 800130
Balch Springs, TX 75180
Phone: 972-557-2887
www.atts.org

Assistance Dogs International (ADI)
P.O. Box 5174
Santa Rosa, CA 95402
www.assistancedogsinternational.org

Assistance Dogs of the West (ADW)
P.O. Box 31027
Santa Fe, NM 87594
Phone: 505-986-9748
Toll-free: 1-866-986-3489
www.assistancedogsofthewest.org

BAD RAP (Bay Area Doglovers
Responsible About Pitbulls)
P.O. Box 320776
San Francisco, CA 94132-0776
www.badrap.org

Delta Society®
875 124th Ave. NE, Suite 101
Bellevue, WA 98005
Phone: 425-679-5500
www.deltasociety.org

Discovery Dogs
P.O. Box 6050
San Rafael, CA 94903-0050
Phone: 415-479-9557
Fax: 415-472-4431
www.discoverydogs.org

Dogs for the Deaf
10175 Wheeler Rd.
Central Point, OR 97502
Phone: 541-826-9220
Fax: 541-826-6696
www.dogsforthedeaf.org

Dogwood Therapy Services Inc.
Melissa Winkle, OTR/L
5028 Colby Court NW
Albuquerque, NM 87114
Phone: 505-228-4650
Fax: 866-904-9976
www.dogwoodtherapy.com

Freedom Service Dogs, Inc. (FSD)
2000 West Union Ave.
Englewood, CO 80110-5567
Phone: 303-922-6231
Fax: 303-922-6234
www.freedomservicedogs.org

**Friends of the Family LLC Dog
Training Specialists**
Francis Metcalf, Trainer
Phone: 510-289-7718
www.friendsofthefamily.info

**The Humane Society of the United
States** (HSUS)
2100 L St., NW
Washington, DC 20037
Phone: 202-452-1100
www.humanesociety.org

Intermountain Therapy Animals
P.O. Box 17201
Salt Lake City, UT 84117
www.therapyanimals.org

National Animal Assisted Crisis Response (AACR)
Phone: 541-953-6316
www.animalassistedcrisisresponse.org

Noah's Canine Crisis Response
419 North 7th St., Seward, NE 68434
Phone: 402-643-4100
www.noahsdogs.googlepages.org

Our Pack, Inc.
1177 Branham Lane, #235
San Jose, CA 95118
www.ourpack.org

Pacific Assistance Dogs Society (PADS)
9048 Stormont Ave.
Burnaby, BC V3N 4G6
Phone: 604-527-0556
Fax: 604-527-0558
www.pads.ca

Reading Educational Assistance Dogs (R.E.A.D.®)
c/o Intermountain Therapy Animals (see above)
http://www.therapyanimals.org/R.E.A.D.html

Schipperke Rescue of Oregon
Sam Ebbert and Bob Grove
Email: Ebbertc@comcast.net

Teacher's Pet: Dogs and Kids Learning Together
www.teacherspetmichigan.org

Therapy Dogs Inc.
P.O. Box 20227
Cheyenne, WY 82003
Phone: 307-432-0272
Toll-free: 1-877-843-7364
Fax: 307-638-2079
www.therapydogs.com

Therapy Dogs International (TDI)
88 Bartley Rd.
Flanders, NJ 07836
Phone: 973-252-9800
Fax: 973-252-7171
www.tdi-dog.org

TOP DOG
350 South Williams Blvd., Suite 150
Tucson, AZ 85711
Phone: 520-323-6677
Toll-free: 1-888-257-6790
www.topdogusa.org

Youth and Pet Survivors (YAPS)
YAPS@tchden.org

Acknowledgements

Iam honored to have heard hundreds of stories from wonderful people about how their relationships with dogs changed their lives. Thanks to all who generously shared their thoughts and experiences. Unfortunately, I could not include all of the stories here, but each dog is special in their own way, with a tremendous ability to inspire joy, love and hope, and their spirits resonate throughout the pages of this book.

I am grateful to Dr. Marty Becker, whom I deeply admire, for writing the foreword to this book. A very big thank you goes to Maggie Airncliffe, for her valuable contribution to the editing of this book. She never tired of my countless questions and endless rewrites, all of which she handled with humor and sage advice, especially when I was feeling overwhelmed. ("Take a deep breath and go make a cup of tea!")

I also want to thank Davina Haisell for her professionalism in proofreading, which played a big part in getting this book in shape; the very talented Darlene and Dan Swanson for the layout and cover design, Judy Kellam and Terri Leidich.

I also owe much to Sam Ebbert and Bob Grove, for allowing me to know the joys of rescuing a dog.

On a more personal level, there were many people who lent their encouragement and support. They are, in alphabetical order, for there is no other way to categorize their support: Rose Agg, Adrian Gannicott, the entire Gibson clan, Gayle Hozack, Patty Staite and family, Yvonne Thompson and Margaret Vanderbolt.

And finally to Emma and Buddy, who hold a special place in my heart, and Haida, my "forever" dog. They were the inspiration that brought all these wonderful people together to create this book.

Joanne and Emma (Photo: John Knox)

Joanne Wannan has written numerous magazine articles, as well as screenplays. NEW LIVES is her first book, and reflects a passionate interest in the welfare of animals and a firm belief in the beneficial relationship between humans and animals. Joanne knows first-hand the joy and healing that animals can provide, having long been involved in activities such as visiting hospitals and nursing homes with her "therapy dogs."

LaVergne, TN USA
10 November 2009

163585LV00002B/7/P